With The BEATLES

With The BEATLES
LEWIS LAPHAM

MELVILLE HOUSE PUBLISHING
HOBOKEN, NEW JERSEY

©2005 LEWIS LAPHAM

MELVILLE HOUSE PUBLISHING
P.O. BOX 3278
HOBOKEN, NJ 07030
MHPBOOKS.COM

BOOK DESIGN: DAVID KONOPKA

ISBN: 0-9766583-2-1

PRINTED IN CANADA

LIBRARY OF CONGRESS CATALOGING-IN-PUBLICATION DATA

LAPHAM, LEWIS H.
 WITH THE BEATLES / LEWIS LAPHAM.
  P. CM.
 ISBN-13: 978-0-9766583-2-0
 ISBN-10: 0-9766583-2-1
 1. BEATLES. 2. MAHESH YOGI, MAHARISHI.
 3. ROCK MUSICIANS—INDIA. I. TITLE.
 ML421.B4L34 2005
 909.82'6—DC22

2005024054

PREVIOUS PAGE, FROM LEFT: Pattie Harrison, Nancy Jackson, John Lennon, Paul McCartney, Maharishi Mahesh Yogi, George Harrison, Mia Farrow, Johnny Farrow, Donovan Leitch, Jane Asher, and Cynthia Lennon at the ashram.

ABOVE: "A banner said *WELCOME*, but the way to the ashram was barred by a Hindu guard, a gate and a barbed wire fence."

NEXT PAGE: "The arrival of the Beatles (here with their wives, Mike Love and the Maharishi) caused unpleasant incidents with the press."

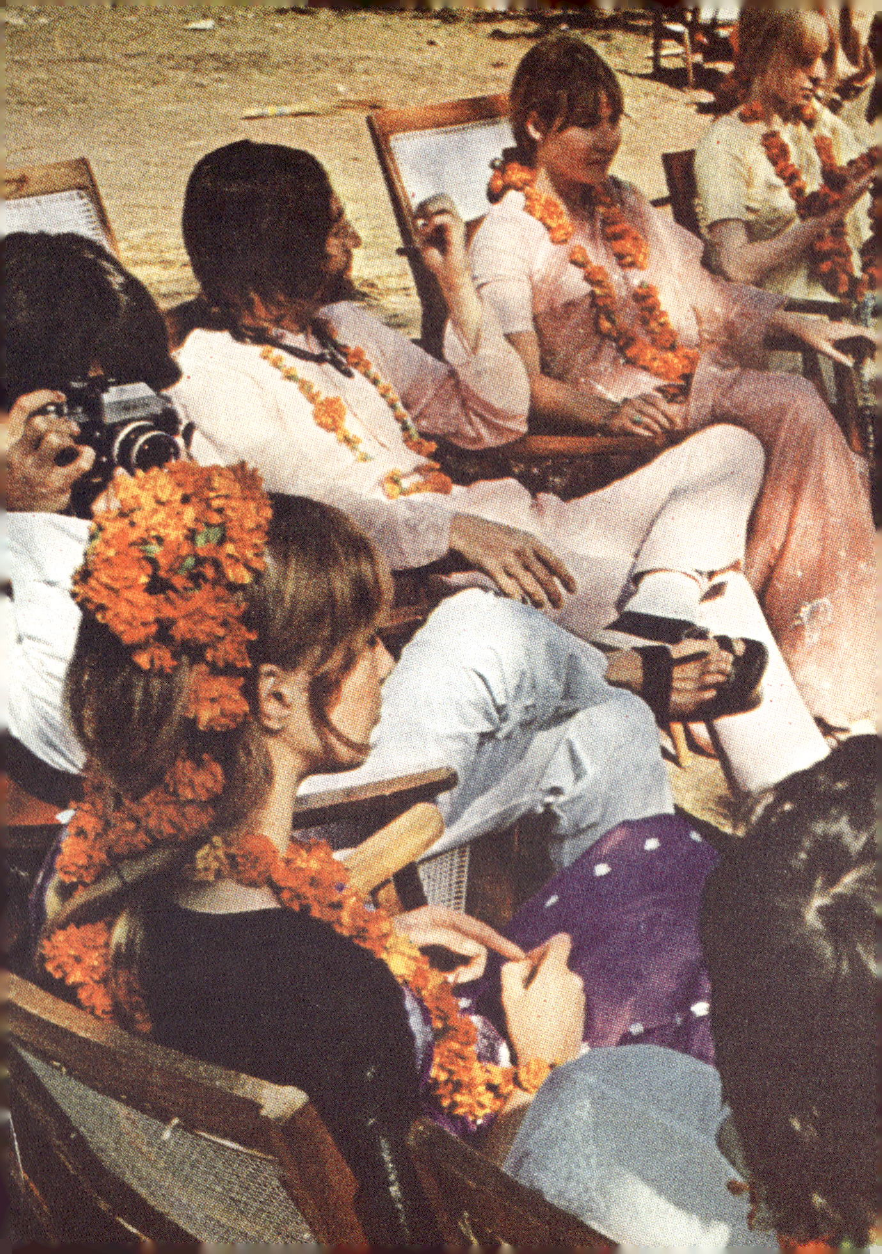

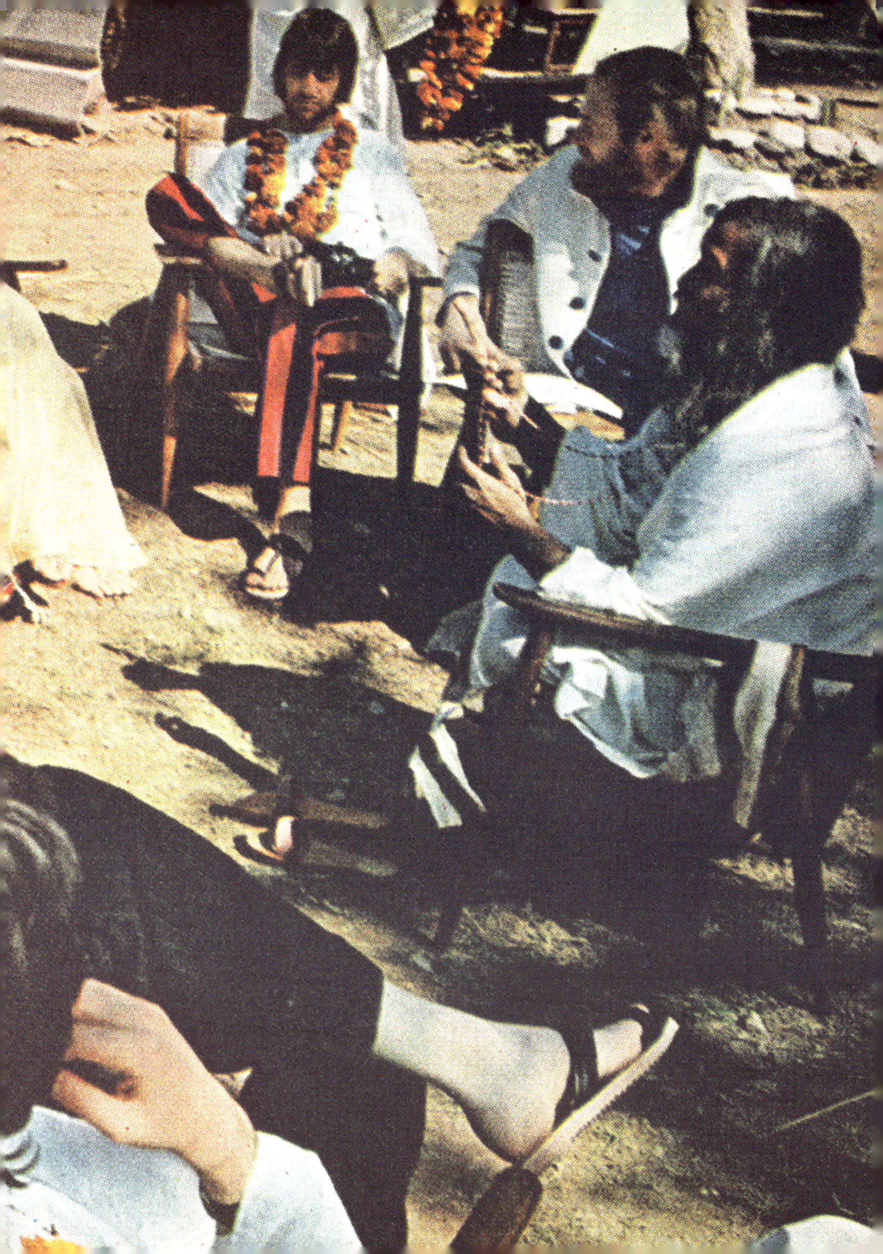

ABOVE: "The Maharishi presented George Harrison with a cake and a plastic globe turned upside-down. 'This is the world,' he said. 'It needs to be corrected.' We sang 'Happy Birthday' to George, and then when the laughter and applause subsided, the Hindu porters laughed and danced and threw firecrackers at one another in the doorway of the lecture hall."

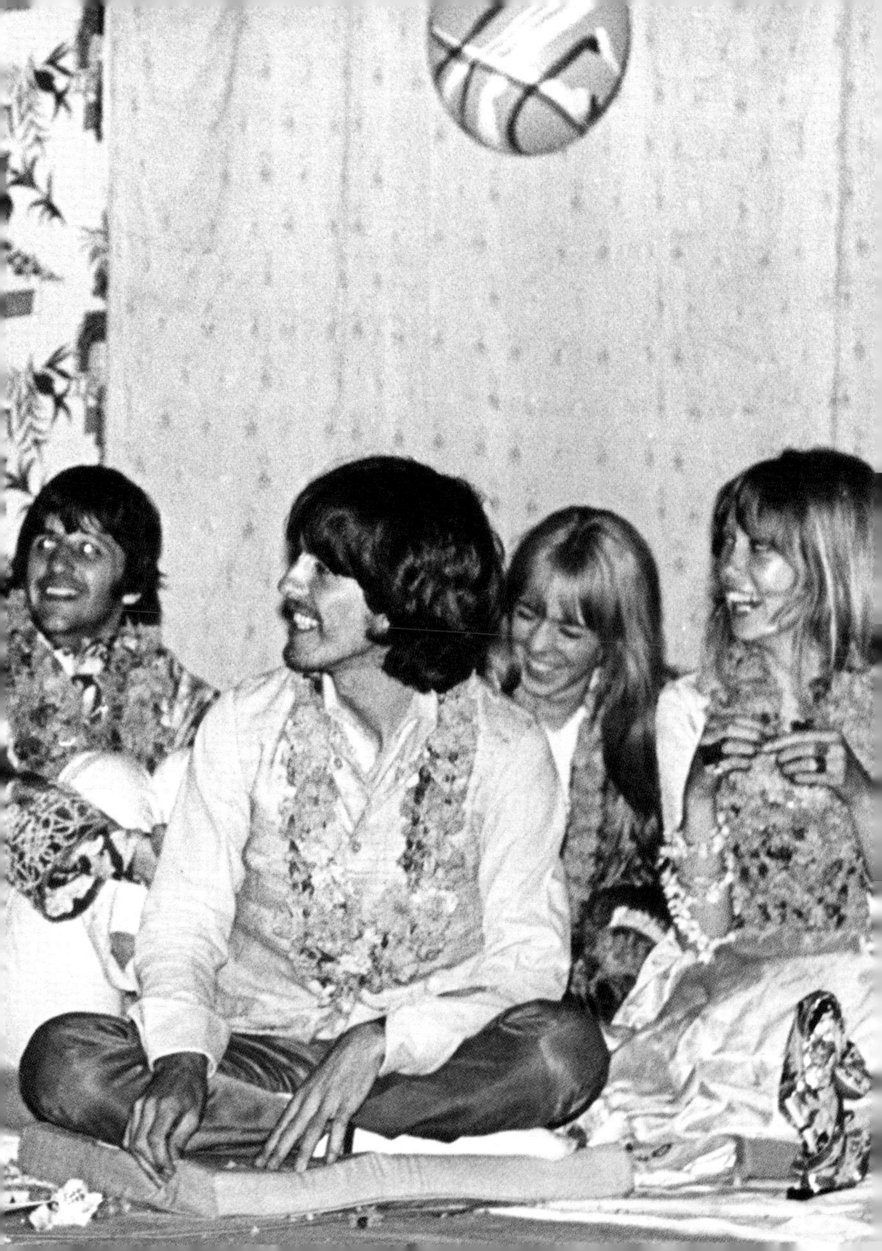

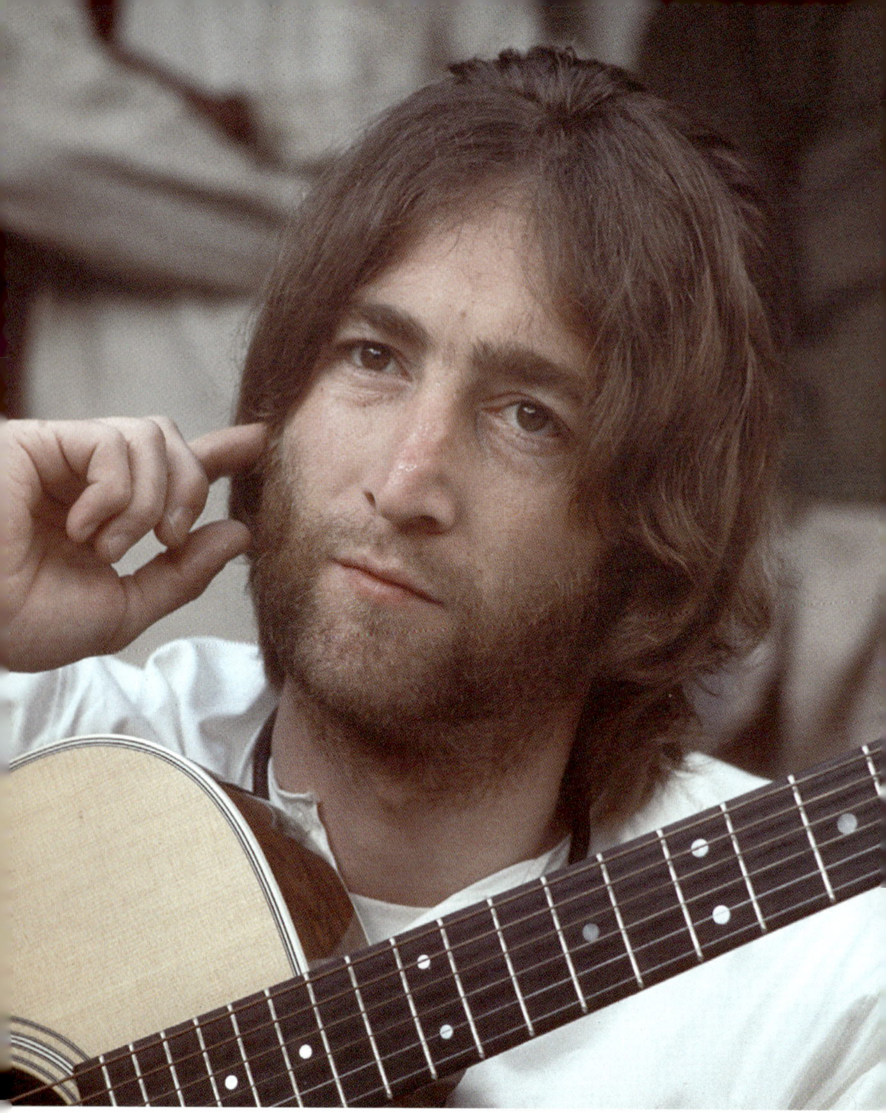

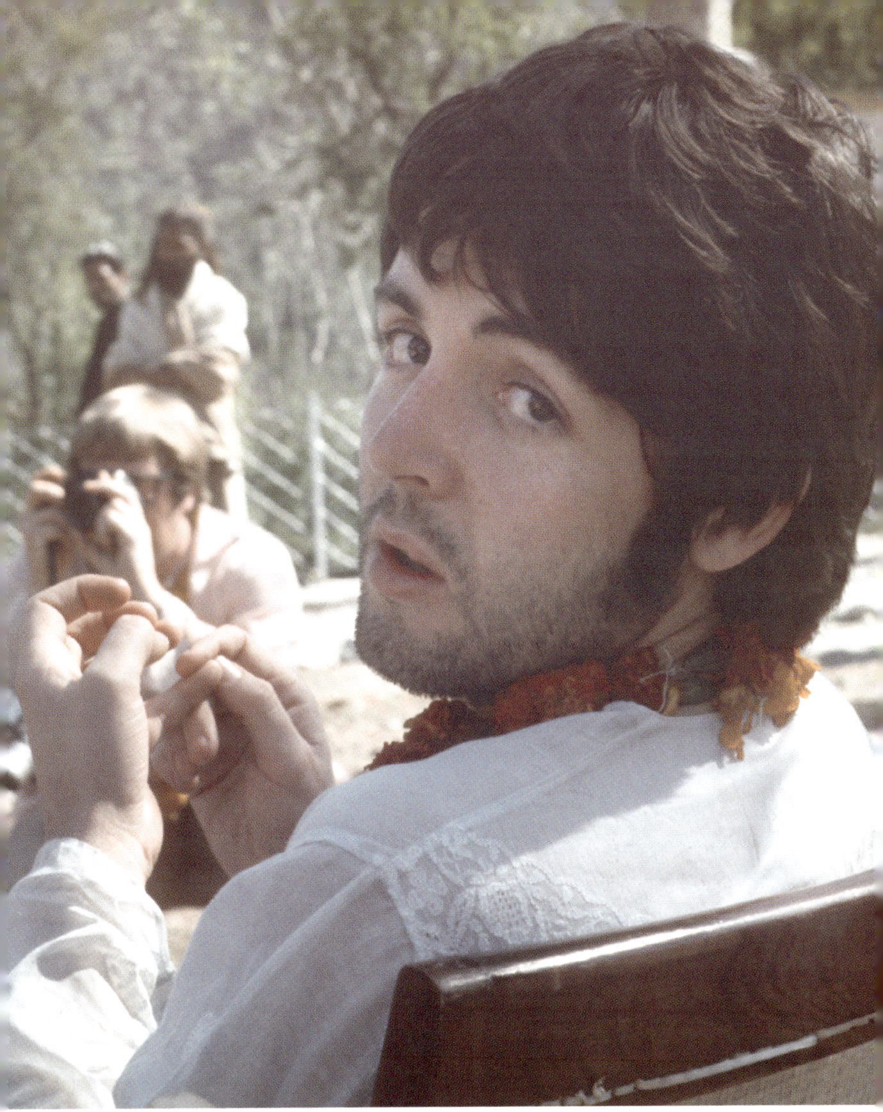

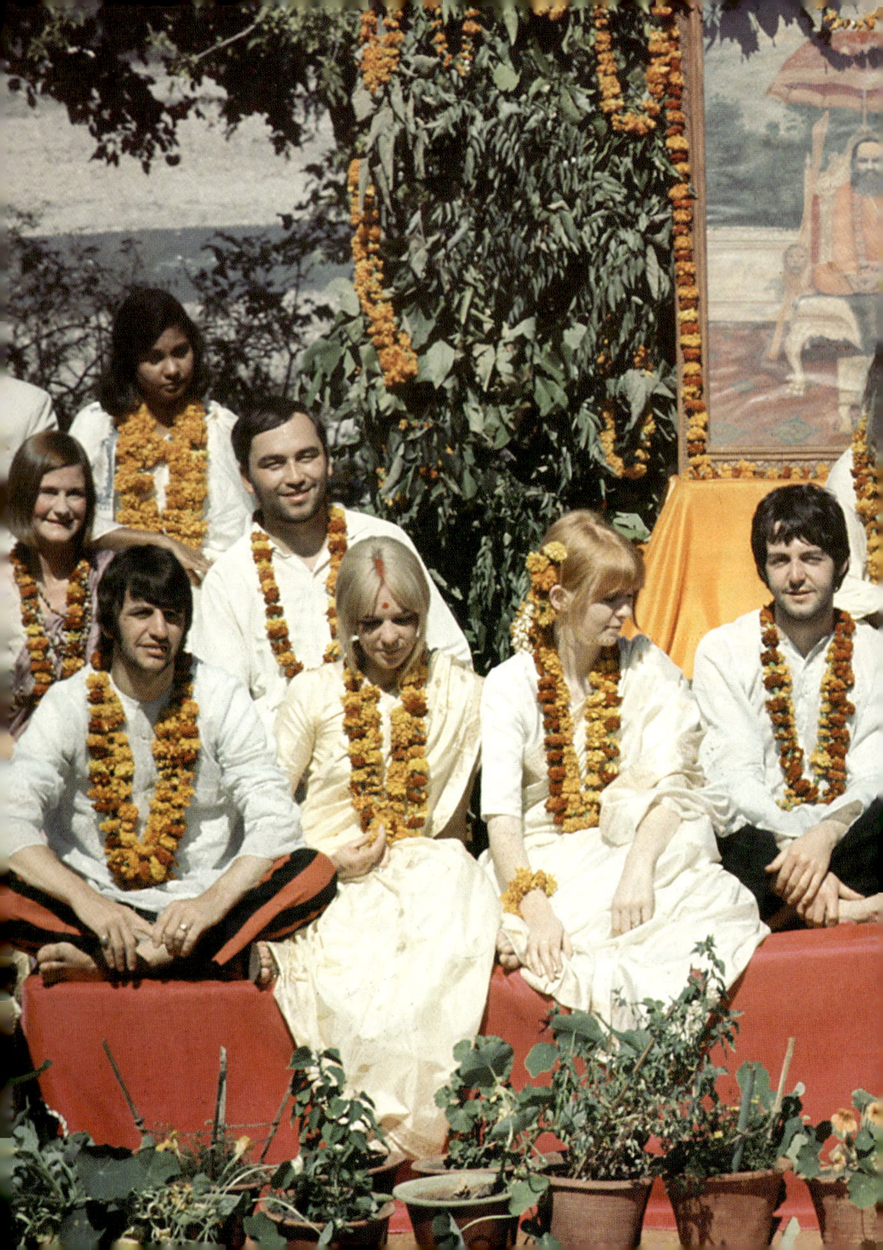

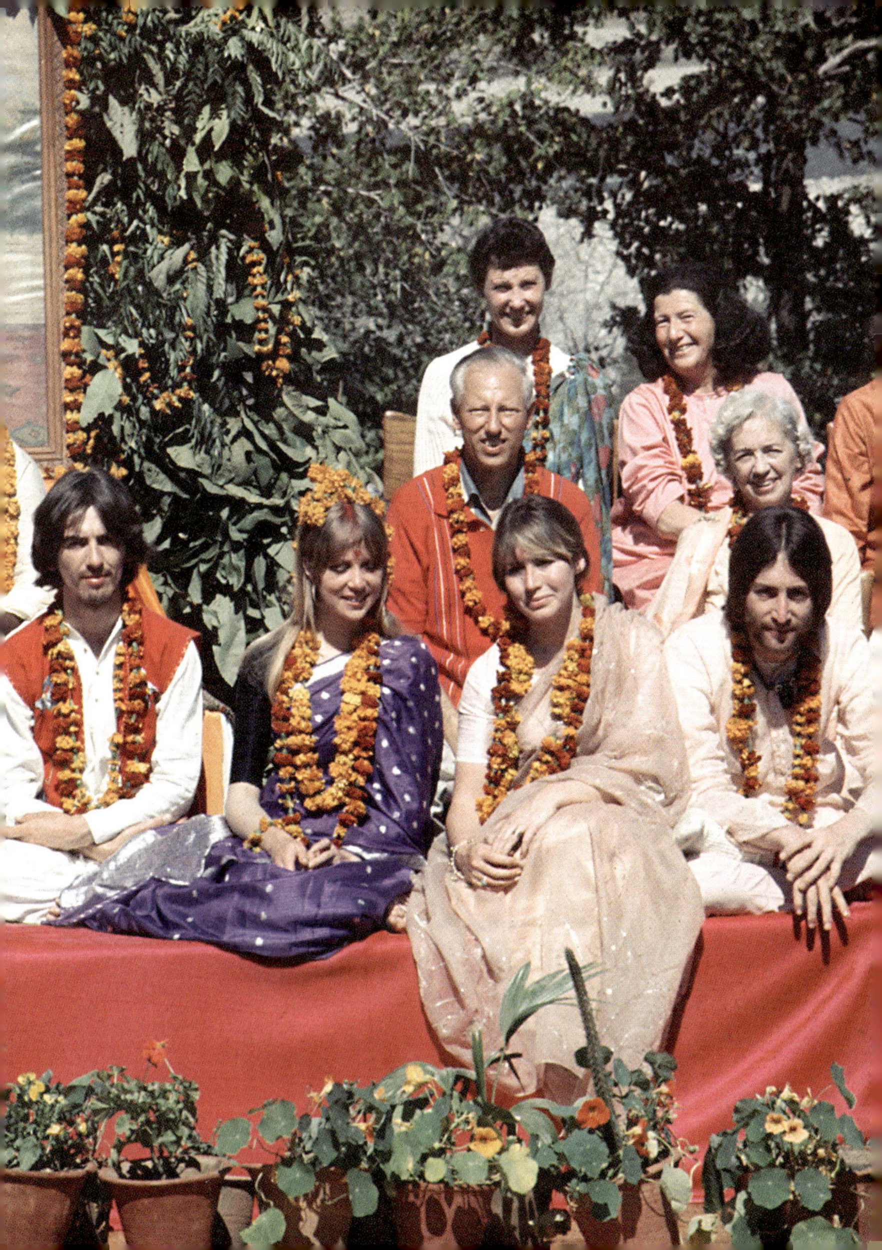

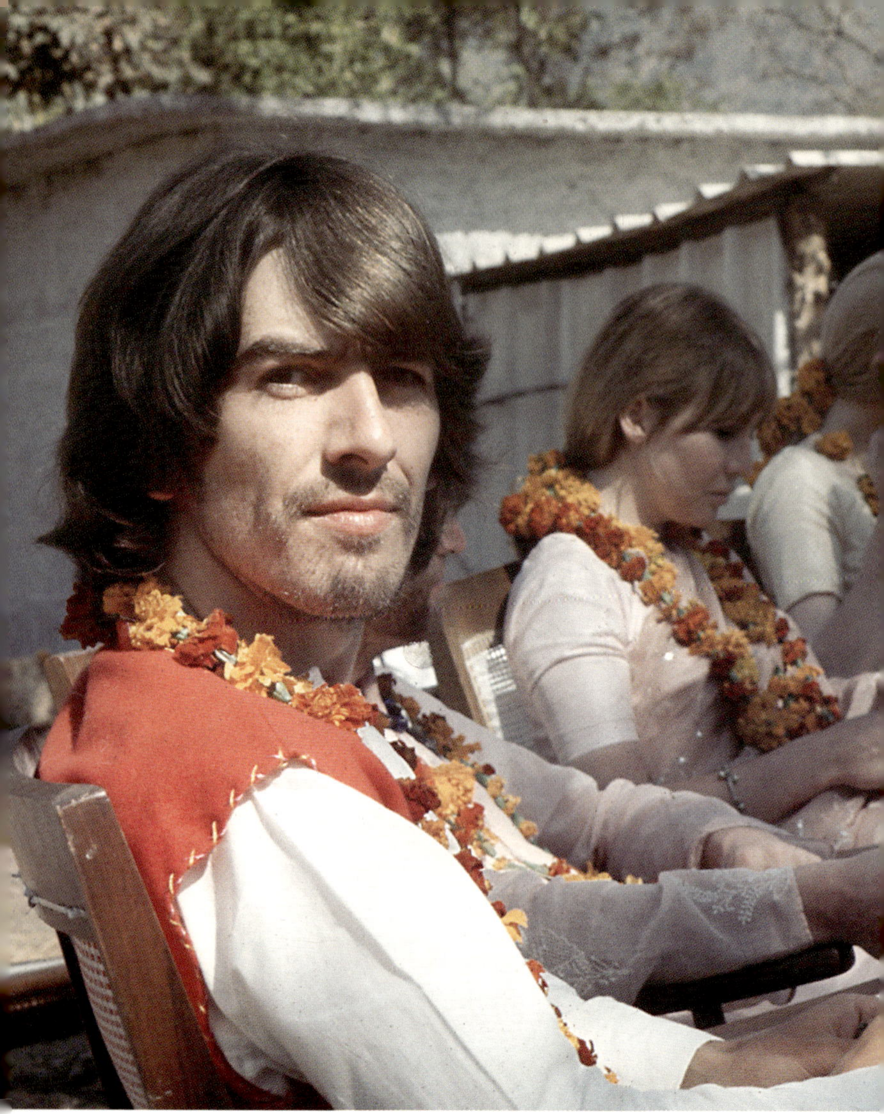

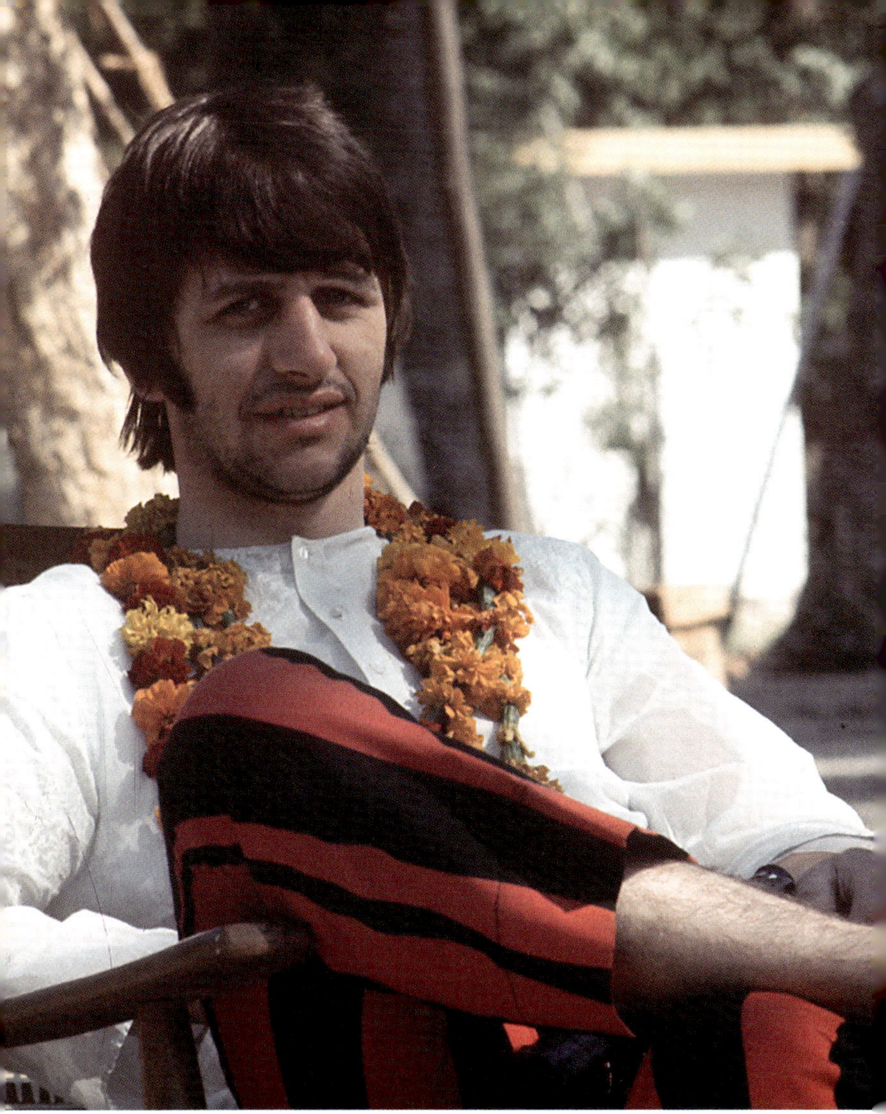

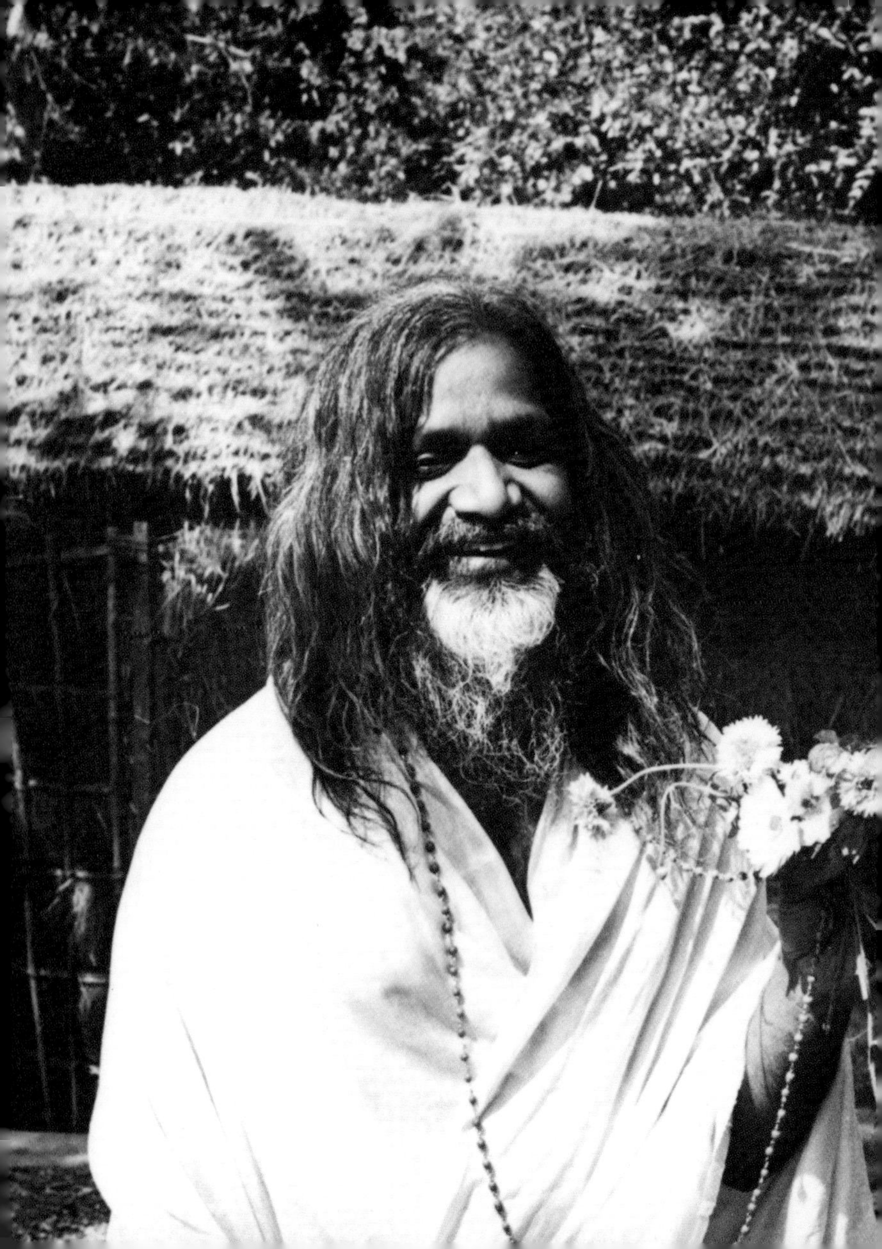

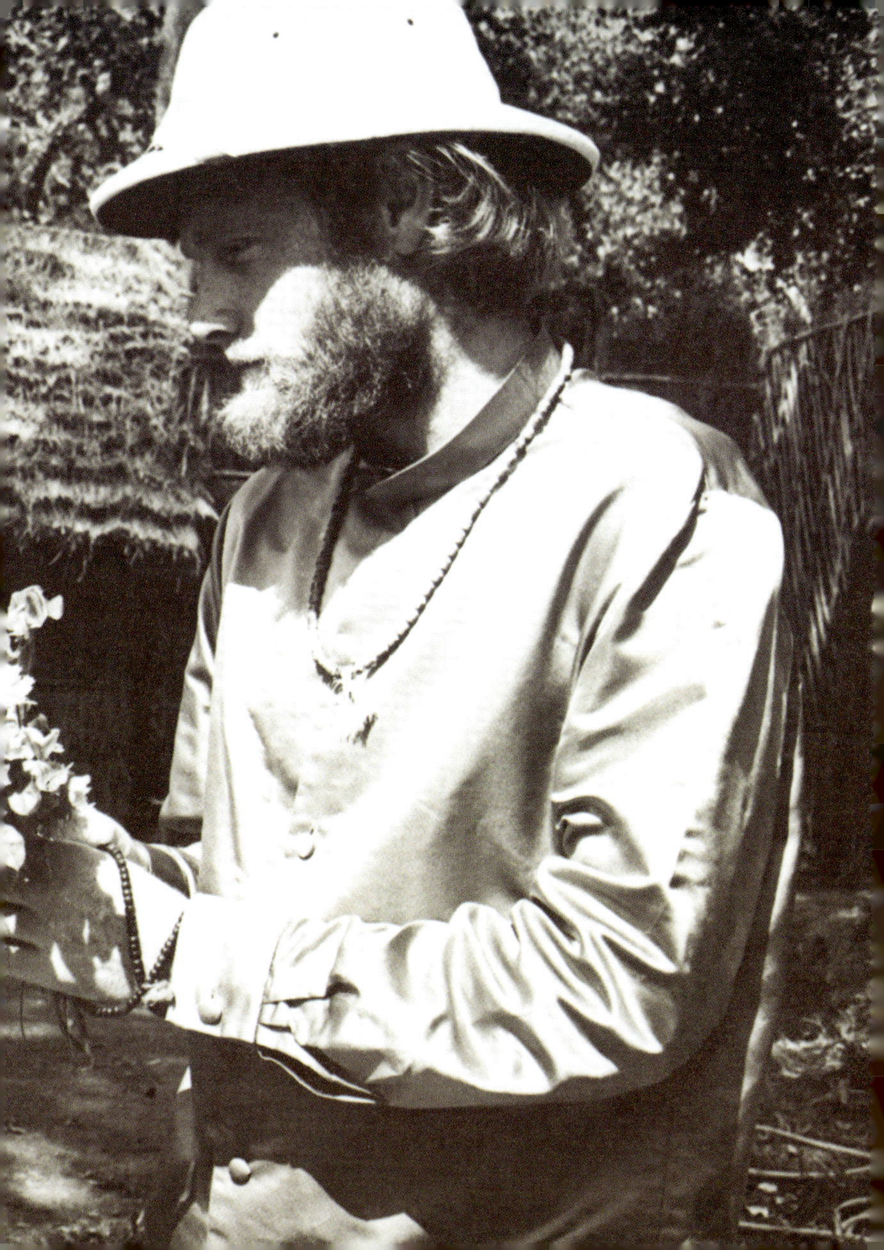

PREVIOUS PAGE: "Maharishi Mahesh Yogi with the Beach Boys' Mike Love at the ashram."

ABOVE: "The Maharishi in his office. He said he admired the American mind and compared it to the flower of the tree, while the other people of the earth were the bark and the branches."

ABOVE: "Mrs. Frank Sinatra, (actress, Mia Farrow) and her religious instructor, Maharishi Mahesh Yogi meet the press prior to their departure for India January 23. Miss Farrow says she is going to India to be a better person. The Hindu mystic conducts an international meditation society at Rishikesh in the Himalayas. Miss Farrow, estranged from her husband, did not say she intends to stay in India, or whether her husband knows of the trip."

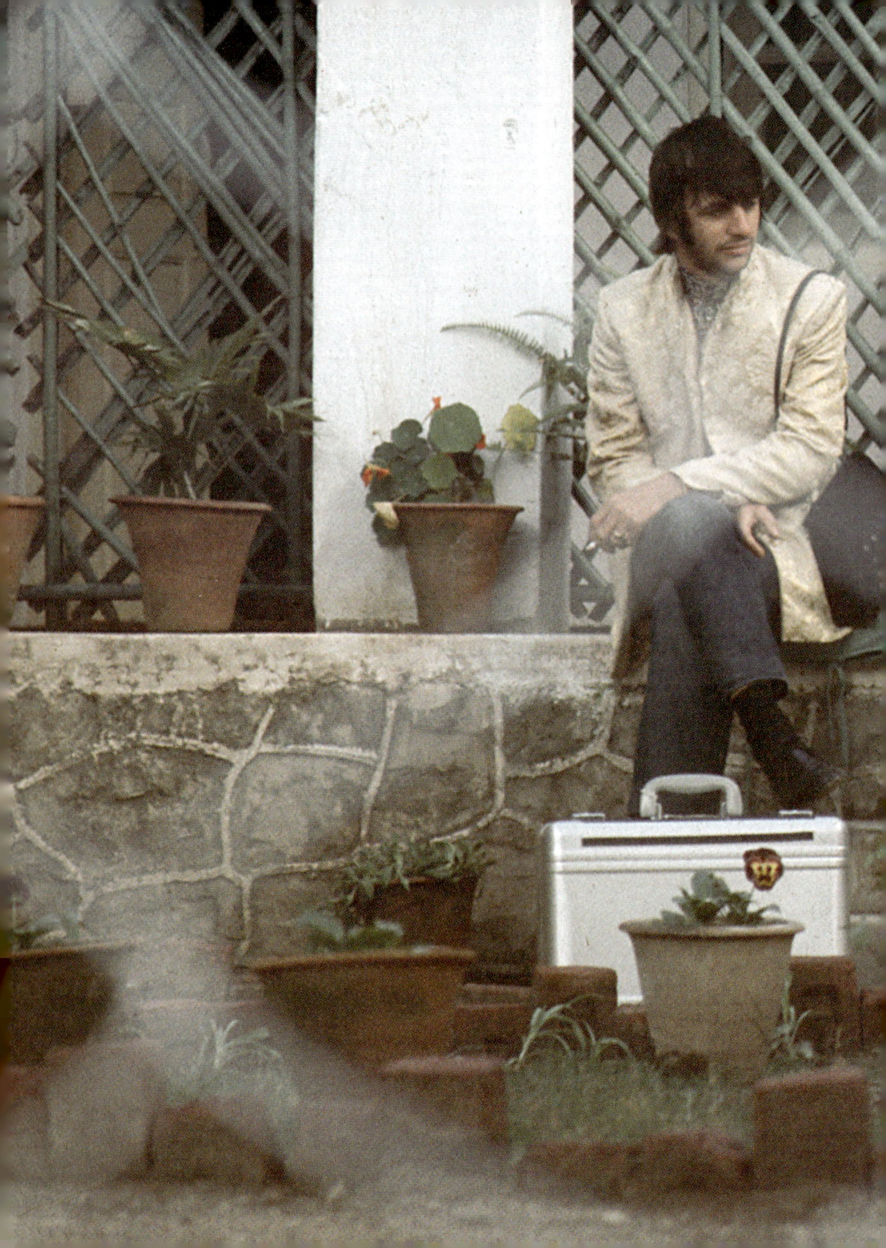

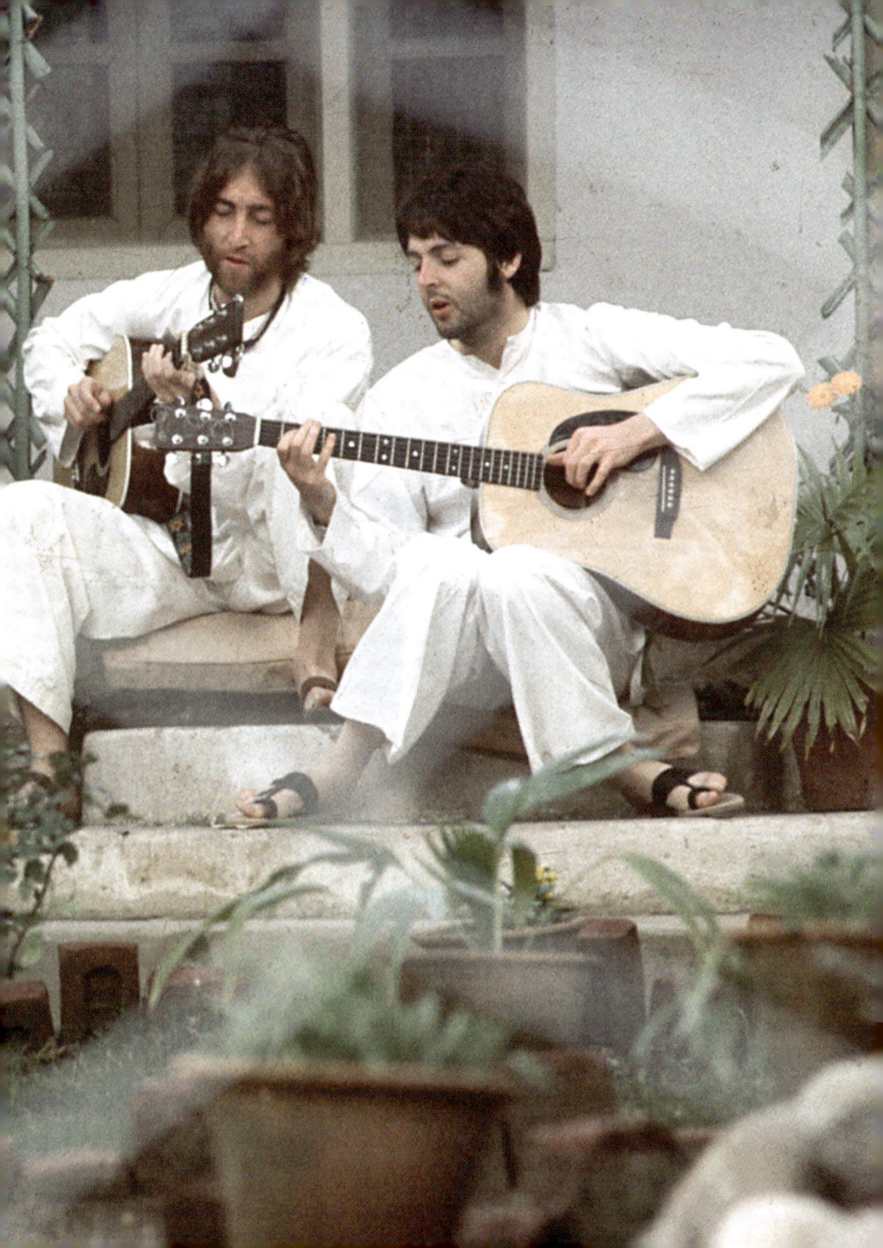

ABOVE: "Nancy Jackson and Beach Boy Mike Love, two of the Maharishi's disciples from California, meditate for the camera."

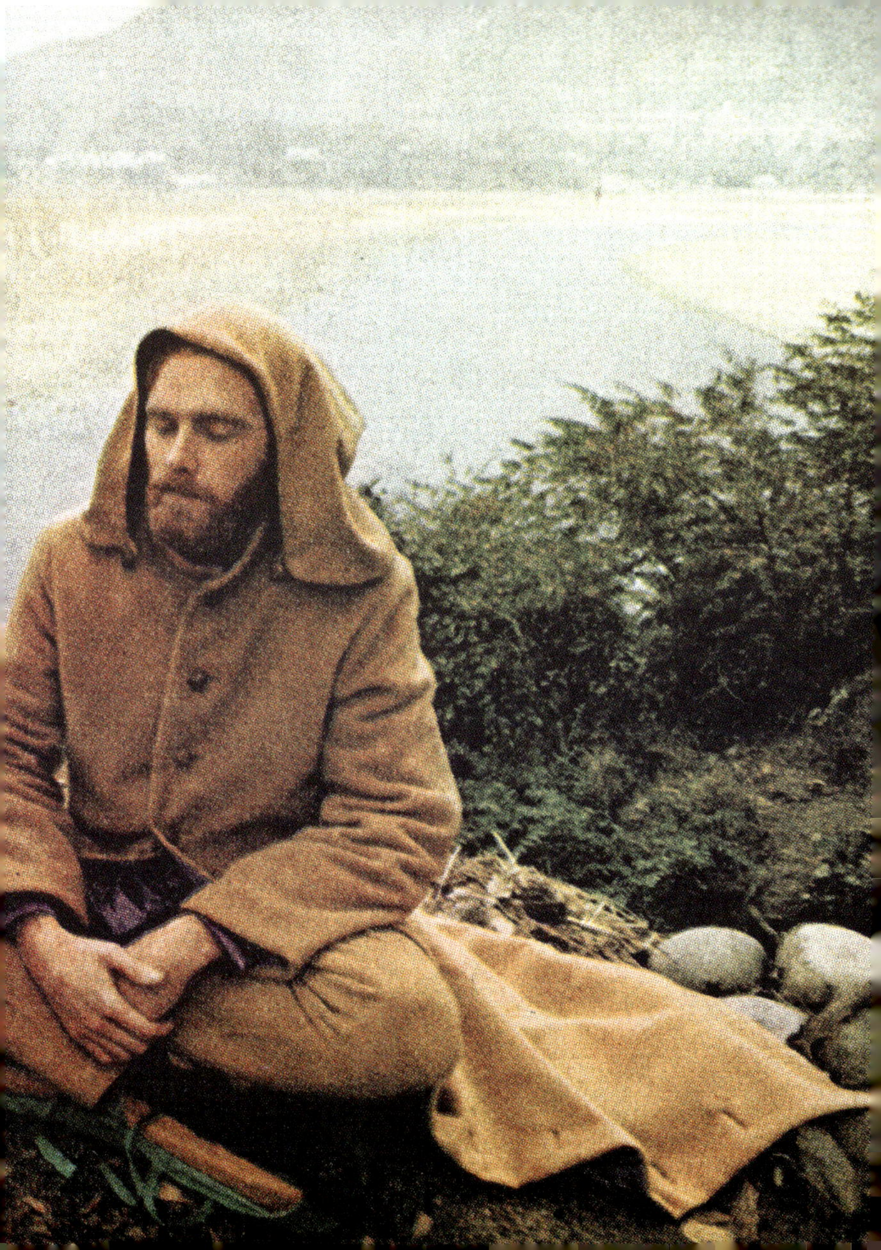

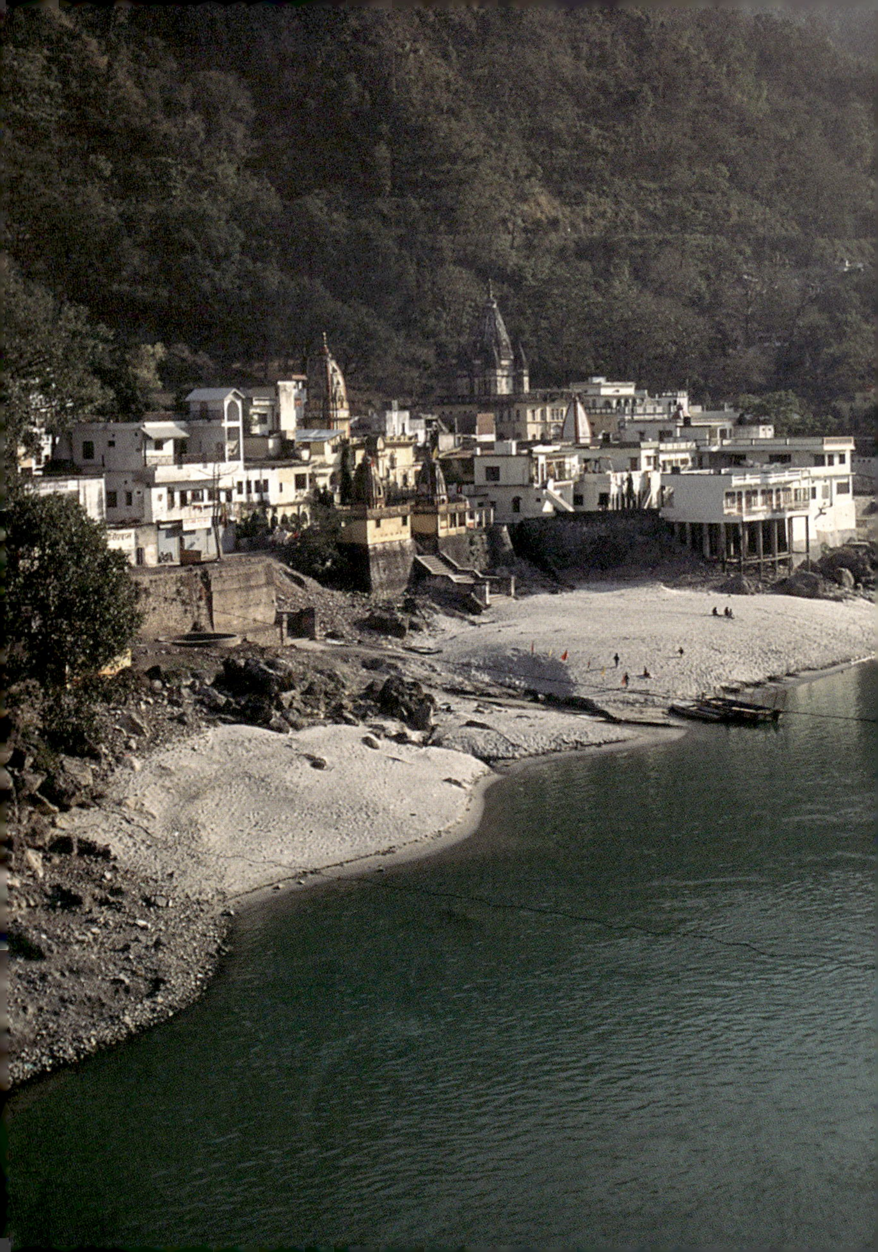

With The BEATLES

TO OTTO FRIEDRICH
(1929 – 1995)
MY OWN GURU DEV

THE DEEPER YOU GO THE HIGHER YOU FLY.
THE HIGHER YOU FLY THE DEEPER YOU GO.

*"EVERYBODY'S GOT SOMETHING TO
HIDE EXCEPT ME AND MY MONKEY"*

I.

On the phone Friedrich had mentioned "a journey to the east," and two days later when I met him for lunch at a Chinese restaurant on West 55th Street, I expected the conversation to turn in the direction of Saigon and Da Nang. The Vietnam war in January 1968 was showing unmistakable signs of an American defeat; Otto Friedrich was the managing editor of the *Saturday Evening Post*, I was a staff writer due for assignment, and where else do journalists forage for the news if not in the deserts of misfortune? Friedrich proposed as an alternative the mountains of infinite bliss. Instead of presenting me with a set of military map coordinates, he handed across the table two song albums recently released by the Beatles together with a newspaper clipping that described the New York appearance, earlier in the month, seated among marigolds and yellow hyacinths in Madison Square Garden's Felt Forum, of the Maharishi Mahesh Yogi. For some years the yogi had been wandering the world with what he called "the message of the flower," bringing to the disaffected children of bourgeois capitalism the sweet science of transcendental meditation. While traveling in England the previous summer he had introduced the Beatles to the technique, and it was their endorsement of the result (hello happiness, goodbye Mary Jane) that had filled the Felt Forum with 3,800 would-be adepts, most of them college students, nearly all of them dressed as if for a street demonstration or a rock concert—love beads, tie-dyed T-shirts, peasant dresses, go-go boots. To the Maharishi's suite at the Plaza Hotel the Beatles had sent a large basket of pink tulips, and within the week they were scheduled to further expand and consolidate their knowledge of cosmic consciousness by making a pilgrimage to the yogi's ashram in the foothills of the Himalayas.

"Where you will join them," Friedrich said, "on the eternal path to enlightenment."

The proposition amused him. The tone of his humor was sardonic; he was familiar with the journeys to the east undertaken by the heroes dreamed of in the novels of Herman Hesse and Somerset Maugham, and he recognized the story as one that usually went nowhere except into bankruptcy or an asylum. The traffic in religion Friedrich regarded as an over-the-counter variant of the cocaine trade, but if the old stories could be trusted to sell magazines, they were hard to come by when the plot line was hidden in a cloud of radiant celebrity, and he guessed that I wouldn't find it easy to open the doors of perception. The Beatles were said to be intent upon a session in the recording studio of the world soul, beyond the reach of all requests for press coverage from the *Saturday Evening Post* and *Life* as well as from CBS-News, the London tabloids, and *Paris Match*. Read the *Upanishads*, Friedrich said, and listen for the music of the spheres; win the confidence of the yogi's American agents, and maybe somebody will set you up with a password and a yellow hyacinth.

About the Beatles I knew that John Lennon had informed *The Evening Standard* in London that they were a bigger act than Jesus, also that the judgment probably was correct. Immense and joyous crowds had flocked to their American and European tours; in Russia their music embodied the sound and hope of freedom behind the iron curtain, forbidden by the state but circulating as emotional contraband in the same way that the early Christian gospels had been passed from hand to hand in the prisons of ancient Rome; in June of 1967, a new Beatles song, "All You Need is Love," received its first performance on the first international satellite broadcast, seen by 400 million people and giving voice to what soon thereafter came to be known as the redemptive and flower-strewn Summer of Love. But if I knew that the Beatles were big, bigger than any country's politics, their claims to omnipotence more apparent than those promoting the American army in Vietnam, I didn't rate myself an informed or fervent fan. I'd seen the band play the Hollywood Bowl in August 1966, listened to most if not all the records, could hear in the songs the promise of innocence regained. What limited the degree of my enthusiasm was a lack of affection for the harmonics of Rock n' Roll. At college in the 1950's my ear for music had been tuned by Art Tatum and Charlie Parker to the jazz piano and the tenor saxophone; the guitar in all its tenses and declensions I associated with fancifully dressed Mexicans strolling through restaurants under large sombreros. My acquaintance with the philosophies of the orient also had been formed in the 1950's, in San Francisco during the last years of the Beat Generation's tenure in the cellars of North Beach. I understood the difference between a sutra and a koan, remembered that the Buddha at Kamakura was smiling at a very cool and inside joke. My small store of information didn't fill in the accompaniment in either sector of the magazine assignment, but at least I knew where and how to find a melody, and who to ask about the meaning of the erotic sculpture that I was likely to encounter on the passage to India.

The Maharishi's spiritual regeneration movement maintained a local outpost in a town house on East 60th Street in Manhattan, and on the morning after my conversation with Friedrich I sought an interview with Harold Fineberg, one of the Maharishi's twelve apostles in the materialist wasteland of the great American shopping mall. A would-be poet in his early thirties, soft-spoken and gaunt, Fineberg at an earlier stage in his life had experimented with yoga and with Zen, but TM afforded a quicker way out of what he had come to see as "the plastic box" of western civilization. What was wonderful about TM was its simplicity. The mind focused on a pleasant sound—two syllables otherwise meaningless but which, when repeated over a period of time and held firmly in the foreground of one's inner thought, achieved the power of a mantra that instilled energy and awakened consciousness. "Like a root drawing strength from the sap," Fineberg said, "like a bubble striving toward the surface of a pond." The man presumably knew whereof he spoke. Having completed a three-month course of instruction at the Maharishi's ashram in Rishikesh (a town of many temples on the shore of the sacred river, Ganges), Fineberg was qualified to bestow mantras on the unenlightened, and that same evening at Steinway Hall on West 57th Street I listened to him explain the procedure to maybe 175 prospective acolytes gathered under the 19th Century landscape paintings and the gilded chandeliers.

The crowd didn't match the description of the one in Madison Square Garden—fewer peace signs and psychedelic rainbows, orderly people in their later thirties, the women in dresses, the men wearing suits and ties, the beards more neatly trimmed, an absence of love beads. Fineberg stood at a lectern on a stage furnished with two grand pianos and a tripod bearing a photograph of the Maharishi in the pose that I'd seen in the newspaper clipping—a small man in a white robe seated in the lotus position on the skin of a spotted antelope, his dark hair falling to his shoulders on both sides of his head, the expression in his face serene and beatific, in his hands a white chrysanthemum. Fineberg's hair was cut in bangs, but he managed to transmit something of the same aura, an oracle born in Brooklyn, speaking in small precise gestures, his language an amalgam of hip slang and philosophical abstraction, his voice so gentle as to be almost inaudible in the back rows of the recital hall. He began with a few preliminary remarks about the blessings of transcendental meditation—the ease of its application to problems both great and small, the rapidity with which it dispelled the worldly illusions of unhappiness and fear—and for the next twenty minutes he presented a summary of the Maharishi's teaching, "which tells us that man is not born to suffer."

"Men live and die in the realm of relative multiplicity," he said, "and therefore bind themselves to the illusion of darkness and pain." Beyond thought and beyond matter, however, there exists the absolute unity in which all creation originates and which, at its purest level, constitutes only truth, light, and joy. The absolute can be found within every individual's consciousness, and by reaching it, for at least half an hour in the morning and afternoon, we can find relief of tension, increased energy and creativity, success in business and improved relations with one's wife or husband. Once known to ancient sages (among others, to Buddha) the technique had been lost for many hundreds of years but had been resurrected by the Maharishi.

The audience listened in reverent silence, as if to the telling of a fairy tale. Nobody coughed; nobody shifted noisily in a chair. At the end Fineberg set forth a few guarantees and conditions. The technique, he said, never had been known to fail. Anybody, no matter how skeptical or stupid, could become an adept in the space of four days. The price of the initiation would be $35 (cash or check) for college students and a week's salary for adults. At the initiation ceremony each candidate would be required to present six fresh flowers (of any kind), a new white handkerchief and two pieces of fruit (also of any kind). Nobody would be accepted if he or she still used mind-warping drugs, neither would anybody in the midst of extensive psychoanalysis.

Fineberg then opened the discussion to questions, which, at least for the first hour, reflected an attitude of reverence—questions about the Maharishi's wisdom, the degree of John Lennon's God-consciousness, the distinctions, if any, between a shot of Penicillin, a Vedic scripture, and a pint of gin. Speaking as if to pet chipmunks in the voice of a man no longer troubled by the sorrows of the world in time, Fineberg answered with the words that over the next few weeks I was to hear so often repeated, in California and then in India, that I learned to recognize them as equivalent to the ritual of Christian baptism.

> Q: Where did the Maharishi find the true path?
> *High up in the Himalayan mountains, where he spent seventeen years in a cave with his master, the Guru Dev, acquiring the secret of spiritual regeneration.*
> Q: What did the Maharishi do before going to the mountain?
> *Studied physics at Allahabad University, worked as a day-laborer in a brick factory, improved his karma.*
> Q: Why is the Maharishi's laughter like the twittering of birds?
> *He finds within himself the reservoirs of pure intelligence, subsists on honey, root vegetables, distilled water, a few grains of rice.*

Q: If a person doesn't think clearly to begin with, how can that person meditate?
Intellect is over-rated.

Q: If the meditation doesn't work, can I go back to drugs?
Drugs will seem less desirable.

Q: Does everyone receive a different mantra?
Just as every snowflake is different from every other snowflake, so is every mantra different from every other mantra.

Q: Will the sound always be mine?
For as long as you keep it to yourself.

Q: How long must one meditate before feeling the effect?
The seed of wisdom grows differently in different soils.

Q: What if your nose itches, should you scratch or forget about it?
We scratch.

During the second hour the more skeptical members of the audience got up and left, emitting discreet grunts of disbelief as they moved toward the mirrored doors. From those who remained the questions acquired a harder edge, expressing the opinion that perhaps the Maharishi offered too much, too soon. From a suspicious man in the fourth row:

"But what is your background? What are your credentials?"

"It's not important."

"But then how can you presume?"

"The same way you will... when you know."

A lady in a large hat asked why the Maharishi didn't give away the secret, as Christ had done, and why tickets to his appearance in Madison Square Garden had cost $10 each.

"Our books are open to the Internal Revenue Service," Fineberg said.

At 10 P.M. he stopped taking questions and invited any of those present who wanted to go forward to the next stage of awareness to talk to one of the young ladies seated at the tables in the lobby. "See Laura if you're on drugs." About sixty people gathered in the lobby, waiting in a double line to arrange their appointments, meanwhile exchanging doubts and premonitions.

Young girl, overweight, dressed in a Nehru jacket and a velvet caftan, "It's the communication, I guess... somebody to talk to."

Middle-aged man wearing dark glasses and cowboy boots, his longish grey hair tied behind his head with a strand of rope, "At least it's a fast answer. Wouldn't it be wonderful if it works."

Second young girl, blond and strikingly beautiful, "Don't tell me if I won't like it. Lie to me."

At random intervals over the course of the next three days I stopped by the town house on East 60th Street to take testimony from various meditators who had entered various states of bliss, and to ask Fineberg a few more questions about the Maharishi's descent from the mountain, the sources of his income, the nature and extent of his hold on the Beatles. The word, Maharishi, Fineberg said, means "great sage;" Mahesh is the family name, Yogi translates as "one who has union with the divine." The man himself appeared in the United States in April 1959, first seen talking to thirty or forty people under a redwood tree in California's Sequoia National Park and then moving south to the stage of the Masquers Club in Hollywood. He traveled without worldly possessions (a carpetbag into which were rolled a few clothes and toilet articles), but as his teaching gathered the force of an ever-larger audience (also promotional brochures identifying him as "The Beacon Light of the Himalayas"), he acquired a suitcase and a Swiss bank account.

About the financial arrangements Fineberg was vague; money wasn't his thing. He knew that meditation centers structured as charitable foundations had been set up in fifty countries; tax-deductible contributions from individuals like those I'd seen in Steinway Hall averaged out at $70, but quite a few people of substantial means expressed their gratitude for the Maharishi's existence with gifts in the amounts of $50,000, $100,000, even $250,000. As to the exact number of the Maharishi's followers, estimates varied—maybe 25,000, possibly as many as 250,000. Who knew? What difference did it make? The movement was afoot everywhere in the world (drawing strength from the sap, striving toward the surface of the pond); the countess Bluchner was building an academy in Bremen, Germany; on Catalina Island architects had been hired to construct an ashram; God-consciousness was falling like the gentle rain from heaven on the neon wilderness of Tokyo and New York.

When the Maharishi's schedule brought him to London in August 1967, George Harrison in company with John Lennon and Paul McCartney attended the yogi's performance in the ballroom of the Hilton Hotel. Impressed by what they saw and heard through the lattice-work of yellow marigolds, the Beatles followed the Maharishi to Bangor, Wales, where, together with Mick Jagger, they spent ten days practicing the art of silent contemplation. Soon afterwards the band forswore its allegiance to drugs, and in late September Harrison and Lennon introduced the Maharishi to a prime-time television audience on *The David Frost Show*. The publicity, Fineberg said, transformed the yogi into a household name, which was good news because it meant that as more people (certainly thousands, maybe millions) found peace within themselves, so also they would project their inner tranquility outward into the disturbed world and thus put an end to chaos, misery, and war.

The notion wasn't one apt to occur to a police sergeant or a politician, but Fineberg was a poet who for two weeks had been pouring out mantras on troubled waters, and if he was to judge by what he'd seen of the consequences, his idealism was not unwarranted. The newly-awakened meditators experienced sensations of warmth and light, sometimes after no more than twenty or thirty minutes alone with the universe, and in the house on East 60th Street several people whom I met soon after their rising from the lotus position testified to the truth of Fineberg's observation.

Young woman with an old cat, "I smiled, and I didn't know why."

Young man clutching a volume of Alan Ginsberg's poems, "What we accept as reality isn't necessarily reality."

Elderly man gesturing with an umbrella, "The good news is that you don't have to stand in the waters of the Ganges from sunrise to sundown."

Middle-aged woman wearing a cape, "No matter what he had been selling, I would have been buying."

By the end of the week I'd gathered what I thought was enough metaphysical luggage to take on the trip to India, but both Fineberg and Friedrich suggested that I go first to California. The movement, Fineberg said, was much bigger in California, more popular and more hip, and I could form a truer impression of its strength and size by talking to college students in San Francisco and Los Angeles. Friedrich was curious about the spiritual reclamation project in the swamp of Hollywood celebrity. Was it true that famous movie stars were taking vows of abstinence and poverty, canceling appointments with their hair-dressers? As was usual with Friedrich the question carried an overtone of irony. An author as well as an editor, he had published a number of books on societies in the several stages of decay (the early Roman Empire, late 18th Century France), and what interested him as an historian was the love of magic—astrology, witchcraft, gnosticism, Ouija boards, Christianity—characteristic of bored rich people suffering from a surfeit of silk and honey.

Six days in California confirmed both Fineberg's enthusiasm and Friedrich's skepticism. I went west on the same plane with Charles Lutes, a square-jawed and handsome man in his fifties, by profession a salesman in steel and concrete, by calling a world governor of the Maharishi's Spiritual Regeneration Movement. Lutes lived in the San Fernando Valley, but he'd been in New York to make arrangements for what he hoped would prove to be the Maharishi's concert tour with the Beach Boys. Sitting bolt upright in his seat and taking no interest in the views from 35,000 feet, Lutes wore a stiff white collar and a neatly-pressed brown suit; he spoke with the fervor of a Baptist witness assigning his life to Christ. "The Maharishi's coming to us," he said "must be considered an act of self-sacrifice."

When I asked him about the initiation fees, he explained that in the beginning the Maharishi had asked for no money. He then discovered that people in the West don't value what they can get for nothing. "He brought them a diamond," Lutes said, "and they treated it as if it were a worthless rock."

The students at UCLA and the University of California-Berkeley interpreted TM as a means of enlarging their perception and extending their personalities. Jury-rigged meditation centers had been set up in fraternity and sorority houses made fragrant with the smoke of burning incense, and the Maharishi's portrait invariably appeared on the wall together with photographs of the Beatles, sometimes also with posters of Dylan, the Mahatma Gandhi, and Che. The newly-minted initiates mentioned "socko insights" and miraculous escapes from anxiety, also the weird but groovy fact that when they were meditating strange cats came to them unbidden and stray dogs fell asleep on their shoes. Believing that "if the Beatles are into it, how could the stuff be otherwise than good," they explained that TM took them on trips much safer than the ones available on LSD; less colorful perhaps, but also less expensive, and a better class of people on the magical mystery tour.

Fineberg's counterpart in Berkeley proved to be a round-faced and sweet-smiling man named Jerry Jarvis, thirty-five years old before devoting his time and energies to the propagation of the Maharishi's message. I found him one evening on the stage of a university classroom answering questions from maybe 350 students, all of the recently turned on to TM, seated in the tiers of an amphitheater. His hands folded quietly in his lap, Jarvis sat on a high stool in front of a blackboard marked up with the formulas and equations that had illustrated that afternoon's mathematics lesson.

A blonde girl sitting high up in back wanted to know what it meant if she fell asleep. Jarvis told her it was a successful indication, that it implied a release of tension and an adjustment of the central nervous system. Another girl asked about daydreaming. That also was correct. To a boy who confessed a tendency to open his eyes during meditation, Jarvis said, "It will pass. There really isn't much to see." Another boy close to the front asked about his own life, which was not going as well as he would have liked. He wore a full beard, a flat, black hat, and a fatigue jacket on which was scrawled the ironic advice: ENLIST NOW—DON'T DELAY—AVOID THE RUSH. Since he'd begun meditating, he said he'd been having a lot of trouble; a lot of terrible things had been happening; he'd been evicted from his apartment and visited by federal narcotics agents.

"What about that?"

"How fortunate," Jarvis said, "that you started meditating."

At Jarvis' suggestion, I presented myself at the meditation center on Channing Way, to see what I could see of the initiations. A few birch trees and a plot of threadbare ivy decorated the approach to a stucco building that once had served as a sorority house. The signs on the door prohibited smoking and praised the Guru Dev.

At 8 A.M. the first initiates began to come diffidently through the door, some of them bringing their fruit and flowers in paper bags, others bringing them discreetly in briefcases. Almost everybody brought apples or oranges, but those wearing Navajo headbands invariably brought mangoes or pomegranates. The girls taking names behind the desk smiled the quiet knowing smiles of girls who help out at poetry readings and paint the sets at summer theaters. The recent initiates descending the stairs with their newfound mantras in mind held their flowers loosely in their hands, as if they were unaware of them, and always there was a dazed and messianic light in their faces. None could explain what had happened to them. Before I left I heard a boy say to his newly empowered friend, "Well, Jesse?... Was it...?"

Jesse opened his arms in a wide and exuberant gesture, grinning as if the other boy had said something foolishly irrelevant.

"Oh, yes," he said, "...oh, yes."

Among the Hollywood film stars attracted to the Maharishi's teaching the most articulate and thoughtful was Candice Bergen, a young actress not yet famous but rising rapidly in the ranks of box office celebrity. On the terrace of her house in Benedict Canyon we drank iced tea in crystal glasses and listened to a recording of Elizabethan lute music. In New York I'd been told that she intended to join the Beatles in India. "No," she said, "Not exactly." She had considered doing so, thought that there was a lot of sense and comfort in what the Maharishi had to say, but then it occurred to her that "everybody was picking up on him... the LSD people turning into Maharishi freaks and heads," publicity agents trying to book him into the Monterey Pop Festival, Mia Farrow cherishing her mantra as if it were a pet sparrow, and so she had decided that going to India was "like going to the Daisy," which, in Los Angeles that month, was the place to be seen by press agents and therefore, at least from a karmic perspective, "not where it's at."

She didn't intend a put-down of the spiritual scene. Not at all, absolutely not. Neither did she wish to knock anybody's search for enlightenment, and she understood, probably better than most, what Fineberg had in mind when he likened western civilization to a plastic box. The consumer culture, she said, everything mass-produced, everything a commodity—not only the cars and the clothes and the hair-dos, but also the ideas and the orgasms. Something quite clearly had gone wrong in the engine of the American dream. "We have so much freedom," she said, "so much money and gasoline," but how many people know who they are or why they go wherever it is they go? The Maharishi's teaching belonged to the happy ending school of religions, another approach to the inner utopia envisioned by the Christian Scientists, Billy Sunday, and Aimee Semple McPherson. Let TM stand as a trademark for having or doing one's own thing, and where was the harm in the message of the flower?

Judging by that week's newspaper headlines, very little or none at all. On January 30th the American military forces in Vietnam had been caught by surprise in the Tet Offensive, the message of the mortar round and the machine gun bullet being brought to boys of the same age as the ones I'd seen in Berkeley armed with plums and pomegranates; the television networks were re-running the recent footage of a South Vietnamese police chief executing a Viet Cong prisoner in a Saigon street with a pistol shot to the head; Senator Eugene McCarthy of Minnesota was campaigning for the White House on the promise to stop the war in Indochina and end the rioting at New England universities.

On the day after Candice Bergen asked her question, the newspapers brought word of a civil rights protest in a South Carolina bowling alley during which a posse of highway patrolmen, all of them white men, had killed three college students, each of them black. Later that same afternoon Charles Lutes arranged an introduction to the Beach Boys, the band then second only to the Beatles on the pop charts and already well acquainted with the mechanics of transcendental meditation. Directed to a mansion in Bel Air (white stucco in the Spanish style, red tile roofs, two Rolls Royce touring cars in the driveway), I found four members of the band—Al Jardine, the brothers Brian, Carl and Dennis Wilson—assembled with their instruments in a high-ceilinged room that served as a sound studio. Dimly lit by stained-glass windows, the room was furnished with a small figure of the Buddha (crudely carved in the manner of a prize won at a carnival), two fish tanks (one without fish), a red rug, three large dogs, and a formidable collection of high-end electronic equipment. The band was scheduled to record a new song later in the evening, and while awaiting the arrival of Mike Love, the lead singer, Jardine and Carl Wilson both testified to their delight in the Maharishi's good news. "To groove it," Jardine said, "you don't have to be a musician, or wear Indian silk or any of that." Carl Wilson seconded the motion. "The most peaceful guy in the whole world," he said, "always laughing, never sad." The band had gone east to see the yogi's January performance at the Felt Forum, and Mike Love had been so impressed that he was leaving the next day for Rishikesh, which probably was why he was late—maybe making travel arrangements, or buying a sitar. Dennis Wilson, seated at the piano, toyed with chord progressions for a new song entitled, "Be Still and Know You Know You Are." Brian Wilson passed the time signing checks, saying that with the practice of TM he found it easier to be alone with himself in the house or the garden. His mother had scheduled her own initiation for the next week; his father was considering a trip to India. "If my dad goes to India," he said, "I'll know that the Maharishi has done his job." When the sound engineers complained of the acoustics in the room, the band members attributed the bad vibrations to lackluster lighting effects (not up to the studio standard set by the Mamas and the Papas) and to the color of the paint on the baffles—not bright enough, no laughter in it, no bliss. Late in the afternoon, Mike Love still not having shown up, they went off with one of the dogs to find a hardware store where they could buy a gallon of chrome yellow and a quart of sapphire blue.

II.

Despite my best efforts to win the confidence of the Maharishi's deputies of New York and California, by the end of the second week in February it had become clear that for the journey to the east no press credential would be forthcoming—no password, no message concealed in the stem of a flower. The ashram's buildings and grounds were off limits to representatives of the news media while the Beatles were in residence at Rishikesh. No interviews; no cameras; heavy

Hindu security on the footpaths. Friedrich rated the difficulties trifling, easily overcome by any journalist who once had worked the City Hall beat in San Francisco. "Be resourceful," he said on the evening before I boarded the plane to India. "Remember Chaucer on the way to Canterbury. If you have to bribe a customs official, set it down as a travel expense."

Two days later in New Delhi I hired a taxi at the door of the Oberoi Hotel, and when I gave the direction as Rishikesh, the driver didn't mistake me for a man making a religious pilgrimage. "Yes, good," he said. "We go Beatles." He named a price of $10, and on the road north—a distance of 128 miles through fields of wheat and sugar cane—he talked about the miracles of western civilization (its movies, its supermarkets, and its cars, everything wonderfully wrapped in plastic, everywhere money falling from the sky like diamonds); when the road was blocked by animals (oxen, cows, a string of camels, the occasional water buffalo) he banged impatiently on the horn of his 1952 Chevrolet, angry at the obstacles in the way of progress ("old news, you see, not modern"), scornful of the beggars squatting in the shade of the neem and mango trees. The journey took eight hours; every now and then we stopped for tea or Coca-Cola in a village made of mud bricks, and in one of them I remember an embalmer seated in front of what looked to be a barber shop, wearing the turban that marked him as a Sikh, calmly grooming the corpse of a young woman before an audience of impassive children.

We arrived in Rishikesh in the hour before sunset, the last light glittering on the temple walls painted with Sanskrit verses from the Song Celestial. From a monastery somewhere in the surrounding hills I could hear the tinkling of bells. The town is where the Ganges descends from the Himalayas, the sacred water still clean and blue, not yet muddied with the refuse of its long and sluggish journey across the great plains of northern India to the ghats at Benares where the Hindus burn the bodies of their dead. In the winter dry season the river is about 150 yards wide; I crossed it on a ferry bearing monks dressed in saffron robes, their heads shaved or smeared with dung, many of them singing.

Above the bathing steps on the far shore, seated against the wall of what looked like an old fort at a safe distance from a row of lepers, I encountered a young man wearing a soiled loincloth, naked to the waist and holding a trident thrust forward at a right angle from his chest as if it were a drum major's baton. I first mistook him for some sort of free-form religious figure, but on drawing nearer I noticed that his hair was blond, long, and vehement in the manner of an East Village beatnik, and that the tattoo on his arm bore the motto, *Semper Fideles*. Taking notice of my typewriter and my city shoes, he rose slowly from the wall to greet me with a faint and condescending smile, and in a voice languid with the superior knowledge of a traveler who has made all the scenes, he said, "You're late, man."

He introduced himself as John O'Shea, AWOL from Norwalk, Connecticut and recently mustered out of the United States Marine Corps. The trident he explained is a symbol associated with the Shiva, destroyer of evil, and as a courtesy to a fellow American he offered to show me around the riverfront religious settlement of Swaragashram. Pointing the trident at the numerous temples decorated with figures extrapolated from the Kama Sutra, he said, "You're here, man—in the Valley of the Saints, never far from the Om." In and around Rishikesh hundreds of gurus were in residence, some of them situated on ashrams, others living alone in caves, and O'Shea figured that a serious student of the ineffable could find a teacher at every level of God-consciousness listed in the *Bhagavad Gita*. A year ago, he said, he'd been working the streets in the Haight-Ashbury in San Francisco, selling acid, reading Kerouac, staying well ahead of the heat. But then the district fell into the hands of the philistines, and he felt the heat moving ominously close to the perimeter of his karma. For the last four months he'd been riding around India on second-class trains, dressed as a sadhu and begging alms for oblivion.

"If you're a holy man," he said, "everything's free, and nobody bugs you about the hashish."

Together with several other Americans, he was living in a farmyard with a peep of chickens. Of the Maharishi he was contemptuous, a mountebank pushing a commercial product, "like learning to play the piano in six easy weeks." But O'Shea didn't begrudge me the chance to make my own investigations, and about half a mile south of the town he left me at the lower end of a sandy path under a banner emblazoned with the single word, WELCOME. At a point where the path turned steeply upward into a grove of sheshum trees, a Hindu sentry stood watch in front of a wooden gate in a barbed wire fence; on the flat roof of a shed marked with the sign, "ENQUIRY OFFICE," an industrious monkey (long tail, white fur, black face) was attempting to dismantle something that looked like a large nut or a small fruit.

It was almost dark when I passed through the gate and was lucky to find the ashram's majordomo not yet retired for the evening. A steadfastly smiling man who gave his name simply as Suresh, he listened patiently to my description of the *Saturday Evening Post* as the most prominent of America's large circulation magazines and therefore the best of all possible billboards on which to post the Maharishi's message. He couldn't make any promises—so many press people making so many inquiries that he wasn't sure who was supposed to go where—but he provided a blanket and directed me to a cell-like room furnished with a bed and a chair in a stone house adjacent to the gate.

Mindful of the rumors that I heard in New York about the Beatles refusing all requests for interviews, I didn't expect to talk to Suresh for a least another week, and so I was surprised when the next day at noon he knocked on the door to say that the Maharishi had consented to grant me an audience. Together we walked up the hill in an approaching storm. Yellow flags fluttered from long bamboo poles set at random intervals along the paths; an occasional trellis marked the entrance to a vegetable or flower garden; Hindu boys crouched over charcoal fires burning in braziers, and in the near distance I could hear the squalling of unseen crows. The Maharishi's bungalow stood in an isolated grove of trees on a low bluff overlooking the Ganges, and although modest in scale—a single story of white brick framed by a narrow reflecting pool—the architectural design could have come wrapped in plastic from a California real estate developer.

Suresh instructed me to leave my shoes on the veranda and to wait in what I took to be the master bedroom—a shelf decorated with Christmas tinsel and a portrait of the Guru Dev, on the wall a map of the world, the bed covered with an antelope skin. Twenty minutes later I was ushered through a sliding door into a much larger room where the Maharishi was engaged in conversation with Mike Love, the one Beach Boy I didn't meet in Los Angeles, and with Walter Koch, introduced as a physicist from Santa Barbara. All three of them were seated in the lotus position on silk cushions, Love sporting a red beard and wearing an Astrakhan hat, Koch wrapped in a plaid blanket. About the Beacon

Light of the Himalayas, I had heard so many miraculous tales that I was disappointed to find a man so small as to appear frail, a vaguely troubled expression in his eyes. His hands pressed together in the gesture of Hindu greeting, he welcomed me as if I were a plenipotentiary sent by the American State Department. If everybody in our two countries could be persuaded to meditate, he said, then there would be peace in the world "for one thousand generations." His voice had a musical resonance in it, and it was his way of ending his sentences on a rising note of near hysteria that suggested the twittering of birds. The sound of the wind banging through the house inspired him to prophecy, "When Ringo comes, the storm clears the passage... in the clear, Ringo comes." Love murmured an obligato composed of variations on the words "yeah" and "wow." Koch foresaw in the advent of the Beatles the great blessing of a sales promotion that "couldn't have been bought for $2 million." He was a busy-body in his middle fifties, pompous and eager to be of help, who apparently had appointed himself to the post of liaison officer between the Maharishi and the cause of world peace. "We'll hit 'em all at once, Maharishi," he said, "TV... magazines... lectures... saturation." The Maharishi smiled and expressed the hope that I could stay for a few days; for the time being, until a way around the rules of the establishment could be arranged with Koch and with Suresh, I would enjoy the privileges of a temporary diplomatic immunity at the lower elevations of the ashram.

Koch escorted me back down the hill, in the rain, exchanging pious nods with the Hindu porters while explaining the work in progress. The ashram operated as a school offering a three-month course of instruction every winter to as many as 100 students of various ages who, like Fineberg in New York and Jarvis in Berkeley, intended to become teachers of Transcendental Meditation. During the day they practiced the technique; in the evenings they attended the Maharishi's lectures. The Beatles had indicated their wish to become propagators of the message—to learn how to tap the springs of pure energy and intelligence not only for their own creative purposes but also for the benefit of others, for young people everywhere in the world trapped in the prisons of unhappiness. George Harrison and John Lennon were already in residence; together with their wives and Pattie Harrison's sister, Jenny Boyd, they had arrived riding on donkeys, by way of the forest road leading to an upper entrance of the ashram unknown to the news media. Accompanied by Malcolm Evans, the man in charge of their security and logistics, they had brought a large store of European luxuries—food, drink, bath oils, and musical instruments. Ringo Starr and his wife, Maureen, were expected to arrive that evening with Paul McCartney and the

British actress, Jane Asher. Their accommodations, more spacious than those allotted to meditators of lesser stature, were equipped with modern plumbing and comfortable furniture. It was assumed that they would stay for the full three-month winter term and then travel, by chartered jet with the rest of the school, to the string of houseboats that the Maharishi maintained on a lake in Kashmir, where, during a second term, they would sit for written and oral examinations. To the best of Koch's knowledge, the program was proceeding as planned. The Maharishi cherished the Beatles as his prize students, and in the mornings he gave private lessons to both George and John. Their wives had expressed their delight in the exotic scenery—monkeys in the trees, elephants in the forest, saffron robed monks floating on the river; in the afternoons they went shopping in Rishikesh for equally exotic fabrics (plush velvet, embroidered brocade, gold silk); from a woman living in a nearby village they received a daily massage.

At the bottom of the hill Koch left me with a word of caution about the Indian newspaper reporters who had begun to show up in large numbers at the Enquiry Office. Unenlightened people, he said, not to be trusted, apt to regard the Maharishi as a roadside snake charmer playing his flute for a cobra. Their misperceptions were paltry, their cynicism dangerous. The Maharishi had great hopes for the Beatles; they would become his apostles to a discordant and deluded world; if all went well and the karma stayed favorable, they might be persuaded to endow the Spiritual Regeneration Movement with an annual percentage of the income from their record sales.

"This is the hub of the universe," he said. "All the world looks to Rishikesh, but it's getting to be like Grand Central Station around here."

That was Tuesday, and for the next three days I remained in a state of purgatory, denied admission of the upper reaches of the ashram but allowed the freedoms of the stone house to which Suresh sent oranges and a reading lamp. Koch sometimes stopped by to assure me that the Maharishi hadn't forgotten my presence, and while awaiting a turn in the tide of events I reread Hesse's *Siddhartha* and tried to keep straight the several forms of transportation preferred by the Hindu deities— Vishnu seated on the primal serpent, Parvati riding a lion, the elephant-headed Ganesha balanced on a mouse. For further guidance I applied to the authorities at the Laksmi Café, where O'Shea and his associates usually were to be found at one or another of the stone tables drinking tea and complaining of the Maharishi's notoriety. More food stall than restaurant, it was a place into which cows often looked in search of sweets and vegetables. A sign on the wall advertised QUALITY FOOD AND TASTY SNACKS; antique ceiling fans dispersed the flies otherwise inclined to settle on the butter or the soup. O'Shea resented the coming and going of journalists that was making Rishikesh as un-hip as the Haight-Ashbury after it had been discovered by the producers of television commercials for the Ford Motor Company, and as an illustration of the deteriorating scene he mentioned a hippie from Fresno named Perry who had been sitting around in the Laksmi when an Italian photographer showed up and mistook him for Steve McQueen. Perry mistook the photographer for George Harrison. Neither of them could speak the other's language, and it was an hour before they straightened out the screen credits. Another of the pilgrims at the table, a twenty-five year old musician from Eugene, Oregon by the name of Putnam, had found his way to a guru who taught him that at the fifth level of realization, "everything becomes hilarious." He and O'Shea had learned to manage their subsistence on eleven rupees a day; in the evenings they began their smoking of hashish with the ceremonial blowing of a conch horn, which certified the religious purpose of the proceeding and thus exempted them from hassles with the Indian heat.

On Wednesday I met some of the ashram's lesser known meditators, who strayed down the hill to consult the tailor and to examine the erotic sculptures on the facades of the temples. The tailor lived in a tent opposite the Enquiry Office and he never seemed to sleep. He made saris for the women, kurtas for the men; the demand was steady, and at night he sewed by the light of a kerosene lamp. The students on holiday brought shards of gossip from the precincts of the higher consciousness. The Maharishi disliked the color black. When he scratched it meant that he sensed negative vibrations in the atmosphere. Meals were served at a common table in a vine-trellised arbor a few hundred yards above the Maharishi's bungalow; the menu consisted of rice and vegetables boiled to a point at which they became tasteless and therefore incapable of awakening sexual energies. The lecture hall, also on the crest of the hill, resembled an airplane hanger—the rows of wooden wicker chairs set out on a floor of compressed cow dung under a corrugated tin roof. In the evenings the air turned damp and cold. Once or twice a Beatle had been heard playing a guitar. Cynthia Lennon had been seen walking around dressed in vivid and trailing silk; she was very beautiful, but somehow she seemed sad, like a lost princess waiting to be rescued from a medieval castle. George Harrison was believed to be studying the sitar under the direction of a master musician from Bombay. Mia Farrow had come and gone. Mia's sister, Prudence, remained on the ashram, refusing to come out of her bungalow for reasons that nobody understood. The majority of the students in residence were British or American, but the Swedes were the most diligent; one of them held the then-current record for prolonged meditation—twenty-one hours *in situ* without swatting an insect.

As to the worth of the Maharishi's teaching, the preliminary reports suggested differences of opinion similar to those that I'd encountered in Los Angeles. The older adepts and practitioners tended to endorse the theory of reincarnation and to attribute to the Maharishi the power of inducing spiritual transformations. Larry Kurland, a man in his early forties, introduced himself as a freelance photographer who had been ejected from the yogi's suite at the Plaza Hotel while on assignment from *Life* magazine in early January. The experience hadn't weakened his resolve to search out the path to enlightenment. He had abandoned his claim to the status of journalist, and he had come to the ashram as a simple novice, glad of the chance to pay $500 for the journey. "A bargain," he said. "Where else can you find

Nirvana for less?" His hair and his beard he'd let grow almost to the length of the Maharishi's, and he was dressed in an Indian cloak of many colors. When he was younger, he said, he had wandered into the wilderness of drugs, where, like so many others, he had discovered nothing of value. TM brought him to a far, far better place, and the Maharishi he recognized as "a cat right on top of the action."

Of the same generation as Kurland, Nancy Jackson was an attractive blonde, dressed as if for an important lunch at the Beverly Hills Hotel. Her manner was brisk and efficient, a woman accustomed to organizing garden shows and museum benefits, and her faith in the Maharishi was absolute. Before Mia Farrow left the ashram in early February, probably because the Maharishi made so much of a fuss over her—placing paper crowns on her head and insisting on so many photographs that it reminded her of a studio call on the coast—Nancy had gone with Mia on a tiger hunt, and simply by meditating together in the blind that the guides had set up in the branches of a tree, they had tipped off the tiger to impending trouble, and so the tiger had gone away.

The younger meditators entertained doubts. An actor by the name of Tom Simcox didn't question TM's usefulness as a technique that quieted the mind, but he guessed that much the same effect could be achieved if one checked into a hospital and did nothing else for three months except read and reread the thirteen-volume edition of the *Oxford English Dictionary*. What alarmed him were the fantasies that seized some of the Maharishi's more ardent followers.

"You're sitting up there at lunch," he said, "and you think that you're talking to a real person...then suddenly you know you're talking to the white rabbit."

As soon as it had become known that all four of the Beatles had arrived on the ashram, the news media laid siege to the Enquiry Office at the lower gate, demanding photo opportunities from the ever-smiling but increasingly anxious Suresh. On Thursday morning he announced that the Maharishi would hold a press conference sometime early that afternoon, and among the correspondents assembling in the Laksmi Café, the collective attitude was, as Walter Koch foretold, dangerously cynical. A columnist for the *Hindustan Times* placed the Maharishi in the ancient and venerable tradition of Indian fakirs dealing in the commodity of holy nonsense and catering it to a clientele of wealthy divorcées, expensively recovering alcoholics, melancholy polo players, bored celebrities—the sort of people Otto Friedrich and Candice Bergen expected to see dancing around the maypole at "The Daisy." The columnist's suspicions were confirmed by the unscheduled but glamorous arrival of Marisa Berenson, an extraordinarily beautiful fashion model then famously and often-seen on the cover of *Vogue*. Wearing a fox coat and accompanied by her photographer, the Baron Arnaud de Rosnay (also in a fox coat) she had come to Rishikesh on the whim of a moment, from Delhi, where she had been posing for pictures with milk-white tigers in the zoo, and where the magazine had been working up a feature story about an Indian temple dancer said to possess wonderful control of her eyelashes.

The Maharishi descended the path dressed in a white cotton robe, clutching a handful of marigolds and followed by a tall and stone-faced monk bearing an umbrella that shaded his head from the sun. Seating himself on his low platform-sofa, he pressed his hands together in the gesture of pious praise, smiling appreciatively at the multitude of cameras in attendance. The briefing lasted a little less than an hour, the tall monk continuing to hold the umbrella aloft, raising or lowering it to accommodate the camera angles when the photographers stood up to take pictures; a second monk squatted at the Maharishi's feet, extending the microphone attached to a tape recorder the size of a kettle drum. When confronted with skeptical and occasionally sarcastic questions about the sources of his wisdom and the origins of his income, the Maharishi responded with gusts of transcendent laughter, high-pitched and merry, gazing into the mirror of eternity, absolving of their stupidities people still bound to the wheel of *Samsara*.

Q: (From the *New York Times* correspondent) How is it that you teach the sadhu's lesson of renunciation while leading a life of luxury?

M: I adore sadhus. I envy them their rejoicing in God.

Q: What is the difference between your teaching and the teaching of Mahatma Gandhi?

M: My field is the field of consciousness. Gandhi's field is the field of politics.

Q: What do you expect the Beatles to gain from their stay on your ashram?
M: A clear experience of being.

When the journalists had exhausted their stock of futile questions, a man who had traveled for five days from somewhere in southern India asked if he could read a poem that had occurred to him on the train. He had not intended to write it, he said, but a spirit had moved him. The Maharishi smiled approvingly, and the man, who was close to tears, recited his verses in the Tamil language. He concluded by kneeling to kiss the Maharishi's sandals, saying, in English, that he hoped to sit at the Maharishi's feet in heaven. The Maharishi acknowledged the compliment with a modest gesture of benediction and then asked if anybody in the audience had seen the article about him in that week's issue of *Life* magazine. Nobody had seen it. "Too bad," he said... "huge picture."

So saying he rose from his antelope skin and walked back up the hill, followed by the monk with the umbrella. O'Shea was standing with his trident in the crowd of newspaper reporters, and as he watched the Maharishi depart, he said, "What kind of scene was that, man? It's the generals and the politicians who let people kiss their feet. A holy man has got to be set to be crucified, right?"

On Friday morning Koch issued my pass to the upper reaches of the ashram, and by noon I'd begun to hear the voice of the white rabbit. I spent the day in the trellised arbor where the Maharishi's disciples, interrupting their study of transcendental meditation, gathered to drink tea, eat their rice and vegetables, compare notes about their voyages on the sea of consciousness. The table was covered in oil cloth, the chairs placed at oblique angles—some of them overlooking the river, others facing the forest. In the lower branches of the nearby trees a monkey like the one I'd seen on the roof of the Enquiry Office watched for a chance to seize a turnip or a crust of toast. The members of the company came and went at odd hours and irregular intervals. Against the damp cold of the Indian winter the women wore Kashmiri shawls and brocaded vests; the men, many of them growing beards, were swathed in brightly colored blankets. Mike Love made a brief appearance in a blue satin tunic and a pith helmet, but he didn't sit down at the table, and I missed the moment to ask him about his descent into the pool of Narcissus or his progress around the circle of fifths. Over the course of the afternoon, however, I met Anneliese and Geoffrey and Gunther, also two middle-aged American ladies arguing a subtle point in the doctrine of reincarnation. They agreed that if it so happened that a person's last thought centered on a cat, then the person must return as a cat. But what kind of a cat, and how situated? A fluffy cat or a smooth-haired cat?

An ill-tempered or a sweetly-disposed cat? One of the women believed that if a person's life testified to a high level of spiritual attainment, that person could expect a happy return as a well-loved cat asleep in the sun. Her friend rejected the interpretation as childish and overly sentimental. Reincarnation wasn't a greeting on a Hallmark card. "You die with a pumpkin in mind," she said, "and you come back as a pumpkin."

Of Anneliese Braun, an elfin and gray-haired English woman wearing homespun cloth tricked out with druidic runes, it was said that she could cure people of lovelessness and head colds by a laying on of hands. She was a translator of Rilke, a graphologist, a poet, a singer of German *lieder*, a teacher of Scientology, and when she first heard about the Beatles coming to Rishikesh she assumed that they were all wrong for the movement. Big time celebrities opening a Pandora's box from which a host of evils was certain to escape—

press agentry, false rumors, grotesque misinterpretations. But then, two days ago under a sheshum tree, she'd met George and John and recognized them as mere boys, innocent and good-hearted, uncorrupted by the devils in the flesh.

"It wasn't for nothing," she said, "that Christ's original disciples were simple men. Carpenters and fishermen, you know."

Anneliese introduced me to Geoffrey, a painter and a teacher of painting in London. A man who looked to be in his late forties, he wore a beard, and his eyes, which were pale grey, seemed to stare off into the distance as if estimating remote perspectives. He enjoyed making learned references to the dismal story of western civilization, and during the first twenty minutes of our first meeting he begged to differ with Sallust's commentary on the Punic Wars and observed that no art critic with whose writings he was familiar had managed to describe the quality of the light in Rembrandt's last portraits. Concerned that I might not appreciate the Maharishi's teaching as a curriculum of genuine substance, he was careful to identify the other guests at the table as responsible citizens—Gunther, the Lufthansa pilot, Tony, the black-jack dealer in a Las Vegas casino—people who knew how to add and subtract, who didn't tilt at windmills or chase after a pied piper playing Papageno's flute.

On Friday evening the Maharishi spoke to the entire student body in the lecture hall, charcoal fires burning in braziers set in rows against the whitewashed walls, candles flickering on the armrests of the wicker chairs, the night air softened with the scent of incense. Behind a bank of flowers and a battery of microphones, the Maharishi perched on his platform-sofa at the end of the hall nearest the river. A coquettish smile strayed across his face when he clapped his hands in joyous exclamation and announced the presence of the Beatles, "the blessed leaders of the world's youth," seated in the front row just below the portrait of the Guru Dev. The announcement was both superfluous and late. The Beatles had arrived a few minutes before the Maharishi began to speak, and their entrance hadn't gone unnoticed—the four most famous musicians in the world vividly costumed in purple velvet and gold braid, their feminine accompaniment trailing behind them in white and orange silk, drifting into the candlelight at the slow and solemn pace of figures maybe once seen in a Christmas pageant or a psychedelic dream. Nobody needed to be told that the ashram had been blessed with a visitation of divine celebrity.

Satisfied with the omens, the Maharishi set about the task of conducting what I was told was his regular evening broadcast. He first asked how long everybody had managed to meditate since he'd last seen them, and when a Swedish woman eagerly raised her hand, he nodded in the manner of a proud and doting schoolmaster.

"Yes?" he said. "How long, please?"

"Forty-two hours, Maharishi."

"Was the meditation harmonious?"

"Oh yes, Maharishi, very harmonious."

"And do you remember anything of it?"

The Swedish woman looked down at her hands in an attitude of sheepish apology. "No, Maharishi."

The yogi assured her that she had made no mistake, and then, directing his voice to the company at large, he asked if anybody could report forty-one hours. Hearing no response, he proceeded to count down the hours from forty, to thirty-nine, to thirty-eight, to thirty-seven. At thirty hours a Canadian woman tentatively raised her hand and to say that she had accomplished three ten-hour segments interrupted by fifteen-minute breaks for warm milk and honey sandwiches.

"And you felt what, please?"

The woman replied in the matter-of-fact voice of a nurse reading a patient's blood or urine test.

"The usual disassociation from my body in the first segment," she said, followed, in the second segment, "by a sensation of intense and pleasurable warmth." During the third segment she'd begun to sing old music-hall songs, the words to which she thought she'd forgotten.

The Maharishi continued his counting. At twenty-three hours Gunther, the Lufthansa pilot, stood up to say that his friend, George, who didn't understand English, had experienced a feeling much like fainting, which alarmed him. The Maharishi pronounced the difficulty irrelevant. "In hospitals they call it fainting" he said, "In Rishikesh we call it transcending." Meditations of less than seven hours didn't warrant discussion, and the Maharishi asked only for a show of hands. When he completed his review, he accepted more subtle questions from people curious about the distinction between "God-consciousness" and "supreme knowledge," wanting to know whether "rapturous joy" always accompanied "the descent into pure being." The answers were discursive and abstract, taking place in what Geoffrey later identified as the two dimensions of primary meaning, at the level of the root and the level of the leaf.

Before bringing the lesson to an end, the Maharishi cast his soft, almost feminine glance upon Prudence Farrow, Mia's sister, seated in the front row.

"And Prudence?"

"Twelve hours, Maharishi."

The answer was barely audible, but it so pleased the Maharishi that he pressed his hands together in praise of the Guru Dev, and then, turning toward a small altar decorated with ferns and palm fronds, he performed a ceremony involving the burning of sandalwood, the chanting of a Vedic scripture, and the ringing of tiny bells. The ritual inspired a good many of the older students in the hall to prostrate themselves at full length upon the cow dung floor.

Shortly after ten o'clock the Beatles followed the Maharishi out of the hall without speaking to their fellow students, the band and its back-up disappearing into the trees at the same slow and majestic pace with which it had arrived. Most of the other guests also retired to their bungalows and dormitory rooms, but as I was to learn over the next several days a small number of people made it their practice to fill hot water bottles in the kitchen and to linger for maybe half an hour at the table in the arbor, drinking tea, gazing at the lights across the river in Rishikesh. That first evening the company reserved judgment on the Beatles. The apparition in the lecture hall had been a wonder to behold, like the album photograph for *Sergeant Pepper's Lonely Hearts Club Band*, but who knew what it meant, or whether it had taken place at the level of the root or the level of the leaf? In the meantime, and while awaiting further instructions, they spoke of dysentery and cosmic consciousness, of poetry and their trouble with the tailor, a blonde and hearty Englishwoman named Edna, breathing deeply and dressed in white linen pajamas, swung her arms as if in some sort of athletic exercise. An opera singer in her youth, she'd found her first week of meditations to be "a ghastly bore," but lately she'd noticed improvement, and that afternoon she'd enjoyed "two hours of perfection... absolute perfection. And then you know that all the rest is illusion, isn't it so, darlings?"

An Australian poet named Michael reported his success in the short form of the Japanese haiku. His most recent poem he'd been writing for three months, reducing a dense sheaf of manuscript to its aesthetic essence, and two days ago while lying for several hours in a hammock under his blankets, the words had come to him as if with the boom of a gong. Asked to recite the poem, he looked off into the distance and then, with a modest smile and almost in a whisper, he brought forth the words, "The Buddhist sat and would not say." The assembled company murmured its approval, and in the ensuing silence at the far end of the table, a man whose face was hidden in a hooded robe calmly poured his tea into a wooden bowl and said, "I'm sure it's Wednesday, but they're trying to tell me it's Friday."

On the heights of the academy the sweet murmuring of the wayward discourse never ceased, and the secular measurements of time tended to waver and blur like the shadow of clouds drifting over water. The same gentle wind blew steadily from the south, and the Ganges kept up its old and sacred progress to Benares and the Bay of Bengal. Vultures drifted high up in the pale sky, but they watched the other shore, and their affairs, like the affairs of the men and animals they watched, didn't concern the students learning, in Mike Love's phrase, "to dig the infinite." Three days passed before I noticed that I'd acquired a pet monkey. Of the same species as the one I'd seen on arriving at the enquiry office, a silvered leaf langur about two feet tall and very quick on its feet, the monkey spent a lot of time in a tree next to the house to which I'd been assigned by Suresh and in which I continued to sleep despite my elevated rank as a particular friend of the management. At first I regarded the monkey as part of the scenery, like a monkey seen in a zoo, one of sixty or seventy monkeys roaming around the ashram, always hungry, probably thoughtless. One morning I threw him a slice of bread; the next afternoon, half an orange, but I didn't expect to see him again. Monkeys come and monkeys go, and who knew what else he could scrounge at the door of the Laksmi Café or retrieve from the Maharishi's kitchen. I misjudged the monkey's character. Once he discovered that I didn't eat much of the food on offer at either the higher or lower levels of the ashram, he became my constant and faithful companion, following me up the path to the lecture hall, perched in a tree overhanging the arbor, never one to refuse a rock-hard potato or an overcooked carrot.

From Paul Saltzman, a young Canadian photographer who had come to Rishikesh with no credential other than his love for all things Indian—the history of the country, its art and its religion, the color of the sky and the character of the people—I learned that the monkey was considered sacred. Properly known as the Hanuman langur, Hanuman being the name of the Hindu god of healing and worship, the monkey enjoyed almost as many privileges as the cow, free to ransack food stalls, at liberty to plunder grain shops. It was a monkey famous for its indiscriminate appetite and respected for its willingness to accompany sadhus on their pilgrimages in search of moksha.

Saltzman lived in a tent off the premises of the ashram, but he had become acquainted with a young and celibate monk named Raghvendra, who was one of the Maharishi's most promising disciples, and between them they could supply answers to any and all questions beyond the competence of Suresh or the understanding of O'Shea. Guru meant "teacher," swami, "the owner of one's self"; Shiva had sprung from the forehead of Brahma, and as Gandhi lay dying his last two words took the form of a mantra, "Hai Ram," addressed to the lord Rama.

Unlike Saltzman and Raghvendra, the Beatles didn't sit for interviews. My presence on the higher ground had been approved on the condition that I not disturb them with personal questions. They had come to him, the Maharishi said, in search of enlightenment, and therefore they must be approached with delicacy and circumspection. It was hard to do anything else. For the most part the Beatles kept to themselves, composing songs or closeted in private seminars with the

Maharishi, but every now and then they showed up at the table in the arbor (usually two or three together, nearly always with their wives), and over the course of the week I learned to hear the melodic lines in the dissonance of their Liverpool accents. George referred to the Maharishi as "The Big M," and of all the Beatles he was the most purposefully engaged with the theory and practice of transcendence. He had come north from Bombay where he and a troupe of Indian musicians had recorded a soundtrack for the film, *Wonderwall*, and he had read enough of the literature explaining the various forms of Yoga to know that the technique had proved valuable to many people over many centuries. In conversation one evening with Geoffrey he said that if he could turn everyone on to TM and Indian music, then he could go.

"Go where?" Geoffrey said.

"Out," Harrison said, "You know, like on a road tour when you leave for the next town."

Somebody else at the table suggested that the same result could be achieved with drugs. Harrison didn't think so. Drugs filled a void, he said, and they had shown him some wonderful sights, but death remained what he called "a bit of a hang-up," which was where religion and philosophy "began to get useful."

I liked his face and his seriousness, and on another occasion I remember he astounded the company with the news that his mantra was a word in English. Nobody ever discussed his or her mantra (to do so supposedly deprived it of its meaning and power), but it was assumed that everybody's mantra consisted of two syllables in mysterious Sanskrit. Not true, Harrison said. His own mantra appeared in Lennon's song, "I Am the Walrus."

Like the other Beatles, Harrison delighted in the costumes—embroidered overblouses, fanciful brass pendants, cotton pajama trousers broadly striped in bright colors, robes for all occasions. They looked like gypsies, their angular faces framed in long dark hair (John's beard, Ringo's sideburns), suggesting tales of banditry in the mountains of long-ago romance. Eventually I learned to distinguish the differences in temperament. John's granny glasses and pale skin, milk-white like the tigers in the Delhi zoo, suggested the persona of a studious intellectual, high-strung and enigmatic, carefully sifting the text of the Maharishi's wisdom for the grains of something that he could recognize as the truth. Like a lot of other people west of Suez, in Europe and America, he'd been expecting a guru to turn up, and suddenly, "There he was in the Hilton hotel." Yes, he said, it was great to be rich, great to be famous, but "we're not the eternal rich men," and money isn't what makes or sings the songs. One evening when Harrison said that "nobody can be one hundred percent without the inner life,"

Lennon told the other students at the table that the band's records served as diaries of its developing consciousness. In the photographs seen on the covers of their recent albums, he hoped and assumed that people might notice "something going on behind the eyes other than guitar boogie." He wasn't sure that the Maharishi was wiser than Lewis Carroll, but he knew that if a person could find within himself an inner wonderland impervious to the pressures of space and time, "then nothing's going to shake my world."

Ringo and Paul didn't talk as much about the meditation. Yes, they had results with it. No, it wasn't a put-on, but their attitude implied that it was George's thing, and if he wanted to go to India, okay, fine, everybody went to India. Ringo missed his children and his nine cats, and he figured that he could assume the lotus position just as successfully in Liverpool. Maureen hated the flies—to the point that if there was only one fly in the room she would know exactly where it was, how it got there, and why it must be destroyed. She and Ringo had consulted the Maharishi on the subject, but the Maharishi told them that for people traveling in the realm of pure consciousness, flies no longer matter very much. "Yes," Ringo said, "but that doesn't zap the flies, does it?"

McCartney objected to the Maharishi's excessive adulation of the band and all its works ("the bit about being the sons of God and the saviors of mankind"), nor did he much care for the abstractions that sustained the yogi's grandiose metaphysics. "I get a bit lost in the upper reaches of it," he said. He also wished that the Maharishi would avoid talking to the Beatles about subjects that he, McCartney, knew something about. He found the Maharishi's support of the draft laws disillusioning; his girlfriend, Jane Asher, often wondered aloud what it would be like to see the moonlight on the Taj Mahal.

Talking to Paul was easier than talking to George or to Ringo—his accent not as strong, more willing to exchange meaningless pleasantries, still fond of smoking cigarettes, his sense of humor affable and tolerant. When he showed up one day at lunch to say that he'd had a dream about being trapped in a leaking submarine of indeterminate color, it was Anneliese Braun who provided the interpretation. She clapped her hands in the enthusiastic way of a child seeing its first snowfall. "How very nice," she said, wondering if McCartney appreciated the great truth with which he had been blessed. Paul smiled and said he didn't think he quite got all of it.

"Why it's the perfect meditation dream," Anneliese said. The voyage in the submarine represented the descent into pure consciousness in the vehicle of the mantra; the leaks represented anxiety, and the surfacing of the submarine in a London street signified a happy return to society and one's fellow men (like Ulysses coming back to Penelope), which was the purpose of all good meditation. The other people at the table applauded, and Geoffrey drew a comparison to the paintings of Hieronymous Bosch.

Every day brought an always-larger crowd of newspaper reporters to the lower gate of the ashram, armed with an increasingly loud clamour of tactless skepticism. Less and less often the Maharishi ventured among them to speak about "the ocean of happiness within" and the "dive toward truth and light." For people with cameras (the Baron de Rosnay, an Italian television crew), he sometimes made exceptions, and on the day when he staged the group photograph, he cast himself as the director on a movie set. Early in the morning he supervised the building of a tier of bleachers, telling his white-robed Indian disciples where to place the flowers, the potted plants and the two new portraits of the Guru Dev—painted by his uncle, a very old man who lived next to the inquiry office and who did nothing else except paint portraits of the Guru Dev. The Maharishi then drew a diagram indicating where everybody was to sit, and as the company of scholars gradually wandered down the hill (the Beatles and their entourage arriving half an hour later than the others), the Maharishi settled them in their appointed places, the heaven-sent band in the center of the set, the lesser figures arranged according to the degrees of their celebrity. The photographer worked with an old-fashioned camera set up on a tripod under black cloth, and when he was ready to begin, the Maharishi said to him, "Before you snap, you must shout 1, 2, 3... any snap and you must shout." Judging the camera angle too low, he said, "Up higher, you don't get good scenes from there." The photographer dragged his camera several feet up the hill, and the Maharishi, turning to the pupils in his school of higher thought, instructed them to adjust the flowers around their necks, dab more color on their foreheads, try to look their best. "Now come on everybody," he said. "Cosmic smiles… and all into the lens."

Even more than the cameras, the Maharishi loved the helicopters, and on the morning they were due to arrive, I joined Nancy Jackson and Larry Kurland in the delegation waiting for them on the shore the Ganges. The light had not yet reached across the river, and it was still cold, smoke rising from cooking fires under the walls of Swaragashram. Nancy had arranged what she called "the visitation of modernity" through her connection to Kersey Cambata, an important businessman whom she'd met in New Delhi at the Oberoi Hotel.

"Oberon?" Kurland said.

"No, Oberoi."

"Sorry, I thought you meant the king of the fairies... the real fairies, I mean, the ones in Shakespeare's forest with the fools."

Glancing every few minutes at the low clouds to the east and south, Nancy made the kind of small talk with which an anxious hostess in Hollywood fills in the silence prior to the arrival of Ava Gardner or Louis B. Mayer. She'd discovered the Maharishi several years before, on her way through Rishikesh to meet the Dalai Lama. She didn't pay much attention to the Maharishi that year, but she remembered that when she and her companions got to Lhasa, the Dalai Lama peeked at them through a rhododendron bush, and she'd been uncertain about what to say. "I mean, how do you talk to a God-King?"

They settled on the topic of the Abominable Snowman, for whom or for which her friends wished to send out a search party. The Dalai Lama didn't grant them permission; he had offered instead to loan them three miracle-working lamas. The idea was to take the lamas on tour in the United States, raising money to finance future hunts for the yeti. Among other wonders, the lamas could perform levitation and materialization, and they could drag the combined weight of seven deranged elephants.

"Fantastic," Larry said.

The conversation lapsed, and then, still in a nervous, gossipy way, Nancy said that if I wanted to write about something really interesting, I ought to talk to her husband, the television news analyst, who had seen one of their friends, an Air Force colonel, step aboard a UFO that landed one night on the lawn of his house in Pasadena.

"Wild," Larry said.

Before I could ask how the colonel kept in touch, the two helicopters appeared, circling once over the river and then settling onto the beach in a loud swirl of sand. Out of the first of them stepped an obviously American couple later identified as Fred and Susie Smithline from Scarsdale, New York. Both in their late twenties or early thirties, they brought with them the air of big-time financial success, people capable of sustaining aggressive rates of consumption. Susie wore white boots, pearls, and a black cocktail dress; her husband, in dark glasses, a blue blazer, and tennis sneakers, was already filming the scene with a state-of-the-art, high-end movie camera. Taking note of Larry's long hair and ragged Indian pajamas, Susie was quick to spot him as a more authentic figure than either Nancy or myself. "Hi there," she said, "what time does the meditation start?"

"Fantastic," Larry said again.

On the way up the hill to the ashram, Susie explained that Fred, her husband, was Cambata's American lawyer, and because she and Fred had been traveling in India for a vacation, Kersey had asked them to come along to Rishikesh. She was terribly excited about the whole thing, couldn't really believe it was happening. She'd heard so much about the Maharish (omitting the final vowel, she pronounced the word to rhyme with hashish); her friends in Scarsdale had said, just before she left, kiddingly, that she ought to forget about the Taj or any of that and just go and see the Maharish, and well, here she was, looking warily to her right and left, as if fearful of snakes or dead dogs.

"Ten days in India and you're not supposed to be afraid of anything," she said. "But you know what? It just isn't true."

In the Maharishi's bungalow everybody sat on yellow cushions, and Nancy introduced the holy man to the Smithlines and the helicopter pilots. The Maharishi already knew Cambata, a follower who advised him on his investments in Switzerland, and the talk dwelled on the arrangements for the Maharishi's flight that afternoon, first to see his ashram from the air and then to survey prospective landing strips for the twin-engine Beechcraft that his admirers in Los Angeles were said to be acquiring for his extended ministry to the poor and sick in heart. The aviation gas to refuel the helicopters had not yet arrived from Delhi by truck, a delay for which Cambata apologized, and so Nancy suggested that the rest of us adjourn to the arbor for lunch.

The meal was not a success. The assembled meditators had come a long way to escape people like the Smithlines, and they weren't slow to notice that Susie had failed to grasp the mechanics of the dive toward truth and light when she refused the food and asked only for a cup of boiled water, into which she emptied a package of powdered Sanka. Fred never stopped filming, walking around the table to set up "great shots" at artistic angles, keeping up a steady flow of breezy remarks that he intended as encouragements and compliments.

"You go to a cocktail party in New York," he said to Anneliese, "and all you hear is Indian music."

"It's very in to be Indian," Susie said. "No kidding, it really is. In Westchester a lot of people are doing yoga."

At least the monkey was impressed. I fed him Susie's vegetables while Nancy, conscious of the awkward silence, told an anecdote about a Tibetan friend of hers who'd sold his yak and left his native country a few years ago to marry an American girl. The girl had met him on a world tour, but when the Tibetan arrived at the Los Angeles airport, she thought he looked strange and so abandoned him.

"What's a Tibetan supposed to look like, for God's sake?" Nancy said. "Nobody looks more like a Tibetan than a Tibetan...if you know what I mean."

After lunch, when the aviation gas had arrived, the Maharishi and Raghvendra walked down the hill in front of a straggling procession of porters, kitchen boys and frightened cows. John Lennon took movies of the crowd of Indians on the beach, the Indians with box cameras took pictures of John Lennon, and Fred Smithline kept shooting great stuff of everybody.

The Maharishi gazed lovingly at the helicopter, like a child looking at an enormous, complicated toy. He absently clutched a bouquet of marigolds, which, when the engines started, dissolved in shreds. He hardly noticed. Raghvendra placed his antelope skin on the co-pilot's seat; John Lennon sat in the passenger's seat, still filming the Indians standing around on the beach with the sand blowing into their shoes, and as the helicopter lifted slowly into the clear air, the Maharishi bestowed his blessing from higher and higher up, waving benignly with the stalk of a derelict flower.

The racket of the helicopters interrupted many meditations that afternoon, and more than the usual number of people showed up for early tea. Simcox and two or three of the other young Americans admitted to being disillusioned by the Maharishi's fondness for modern technology. Like O'Shea, they'd come prepared to live on roots and berries, to bathe in the Ganges, to wash away their stupidity and pride in the ponds of pure intellect and awakened consciousness. The meditation they still thought helpful, but they found themselves spending less time alone in their rooms, falling back on the support of alcohol and tobacco, talking more often about the pleasures synonymous with Santa Monica Boulevard. Mike Love had taken to wearing a deerstalker hat, and he didn't mind saying that stray sexual images sometimes intruded upon his contemplation of the infinite. "On a very gross level of vibrations, man," he said. "The only thing that keeps me going is the thought of a Max's sandwich at the Stage."

On the night the balloons appeared in the lecture hall, Geoffrey mistook them for decorations in honor of Shiva's marriage to Parvati, a supposition apparently confirmed by the presence of the Indian musicians on the stage, among them a Sikh wearing a turban and gold slippers that curled at the toes.

"How nice," Geoffrey said. "Shiva day."

He spoke of the water flowing from Shiva's head (the ultimate source of the river Ganga), which so pleased him that he didn't mind when it turned out that he was wrong about the balloons. Together with the musicians, they'd been ordered for the celebration of George Harrison's birthday. The Beatles and their entourage sat on cushions to one side of the Maharishi's platform sofa while a pundit from Rishikesh, himself a wise man of wide reputation, began a lyrical Hindu chant. The Maharishi affectionately stroked the hair on Harrison's head; Raghvendra crawled around the stage on his knees, dabbing yellowish smudges of ocher mixed with saffron on the foreheads of the Beatles and their wives.

"To cool the nervous system," Geoffrey said.

The chant ended on the sustained and diminishing sound of a single note plucked from a stringed instrument, its disappearance marked by the faint tapping on a drum. The Maharishi then asked if there were any songs that anybody wished to sing. The Beatles let the moment pass, but Mike Love attempted an improvisation, a capella and without benefit of a microphone. "If Transcendental Meditation *can*, emancipate the *man*...." He couldn't get any further with it, and the Maharishi filled in with a soliloquy in the key of C major, his voice more musical than I'd ever heard it, his head tilted to one side at the angle of a quizzical bird listening for a sound or scouting for a seed. Edna moved among the students seated with their candles in the wicker chairs, handing each of us a garland of wet, fresh marigolds.

"To give to George," she said.

There was a good time coming, the Maharishi said, the rebirth of mankind on the bank of the sacred river, Ganges. Ever since he'd seen George Harrison and his blessed friends, he'd known that a great new hope was abroad in the world, that his movement must succeed, that men would no longer suffer. Angels were vibrating with the good news; great prophets in different lands and hemispheres were sending the same message, that on George Harrison's twenty-fifth birthday, all creation had been awakened to the certain promise of bliss eternal.

After the Maharishi had concluded his remarks, we all walked up onto the stage and draped the orange flowers around Harrison's neck, so many of them that he looked like a man wearing a life jacket. Embarrassed by the weight of the flattery, he smiled awkwardly and said, "It's not me, you know." The Maharishi presented him with a cake and a plastic globe turned upside-down. "This is the world," he said. "It needs to be corrected." We sang "Happy Birthday" to George, and then when the laughter and applause subsided, the Hindu porters laughed and danced and threw firecrackers at one another in the doorway of the lecture hall.

Donovan arrived toward evening of the next day, walking up the sandy path with his friend Gypsy Dave, his guitar over his shoulder and a cigarette drooping from the corner of this mouth, in time to listen later that night to another group of Indian musicians play a sequence of ragas. At the end of the performance, Ringo and Maureen stood in line with everybody else to fill their hot water bottles from the pots in the kitchen. Donovan and Harrison stayed long enough at the table under the trees to share a pot of tea and discuss the sound that all of us had heard.

"It built," Donovan said.

"It's rock," George said, "That's what it is."

Everybody smiled, glad to have been present for an exchange of views at the highest levels of authority, and there followed a general agreement that the ragas had been a groove. Harrison mentioned his idea about earplugs replacing record players (so that people could hear the music better), also his notion of an academy that the Beatles hoped to build for the Maharishi in London. Taking account of "the tax deductions for that sort of thing," he figured that the band could raise the construction money from the proceeds of a single concert. He envisioned a large and colorful place where the kids could dance, sing, meditate, and maybe find their way around the fear of life and death. Donovan spoke so softly that it was hard to hear what he said, the expression in his face as sweet and vulnerable as that of a lost child. He said that he meditated in the hour before his concerts to settle his mind and improve his performance; the kids in the

United States he thought very beautiful, in search of spiritual peace instead of a cheap sensation in the pit of their stomachs.

In the morning it rained, and Mia Farrow came back. She appeared at lunch, wearing white, loose-fitting cotton pajamas and gold-rimmed glasses. Telling her story to John Lennon, she said she'd been to Goa, and there, with her brother, she'd bought a stove for a few rupees and lived for a week on the beach.

"You've got to do it right, to be with the people and never mind the rotten conditions," she said. "Otherwise you've missed the magic of that magical land."

From Delhi she'd traveled all night on a third-class train—wooden benches, no electric light, odd animals. She spoke to Lennon as an equal, another luminous avatar accustomed to the thin air on the high plateau of fame, the light much brighter than in the valleys of anonymity. They'd had "all of it" at a young age, but what was it worth, and what did it mean? Even with jewels and your name in the papers, who wanted to live with silly, artificial rules in the "boxed-in generation" among people who insisted on "putting everything in bags."

Later that afternoon, watching the rain squalls chasing each other across the currents in the river, she addressed her remarks to the company at large, saying that she regarded her term on the ashram as "a romp," like being a kid again. She liked to roam in the forest and listen to the screaming of the wild peacocks.

"I'm flying from flower to flower," she said, "looking for a place where people will let me be."

She said nothing about the tiger hunt, or about her reasons for leaving the ashram a few weeks before. The Maharishi had been glad to have her back, and he had restored her to a place in the front row with Donovan, the Beatles, and Mike Love. George had promised to teach her how to play the guitar, but not yet because in a few days she had to go to London to shoot a movie with Elizabeth Taylor. On the far shore of the Ganges we could see a bullock dragging a cart loaded with sugarcane; midstream, a ferry bringing from Rishikesh a company of sadhus seated in a row of white loincloths under black umbrellas.

Toward the end of the last week in February it began to be whispered in some quarters of the Ashram that the Maharishi had broken his vow of celibacy. Nobody was in possession of any facts; different sources floated different rumors—the Maharishi advancing on an Australian nurse, the Maharishi like Jove in the guise of a swan, descending on the person of a California coed—but the rumors alarmed the Beatles. They had made a hard day's journey to the pure spring of spiritual love flowing from the wells of wisdom in the Himalayas, and what if it turned out that the sacred water was polluted with the weed of lust?

Very bad karma for the Maharishi and the band. The British press would laugh them to scorn, discredit their songs, play them for suckers. The Indian newspaper correspondents grumbling at the lower gate already were imagining licentious revels under the ashram's canopy of trees, and what if the envious slanders were proven true? Ringo dismissed the gossip as nonsense, but it provided him with a reason to make good his escape from the Garden of Eden, and on the day that the Maharishi assigned Raghvendra to escort him to New Delhi, it was suggested by Walter Koch that I share the ride.

I didn't need to be asked twice. Every night for ten nights by the light of Suresh's kerosene lamp, I'd been setting up the day's notes into what had become sixty-eight pages of typescript, and although I couldn't pretend to an understanding of all the lyrics of "Lucy in the Sky with Diamonds," I didn't think it likely that in another twenty or thirty days I would discover the secret of Paul's musical genius, the logic of John's irony, the reasons for Cynthia's unhappiness. Nor was I apt to solve the puzzle of Mia Farrow or guess correctly the style and slant of Mike Love's next hat. On walking out the door of the stone house with my typewriter and traveling bag, I knew I would find the sacred monkey standing in a nearby tree—ever watchful, always hungry, *semper fideles*—and before walking up the path to the Maharishi's bungalow, I gave him what remained of my food stores (two oranges, six peanut butter crackers, a wedge of processed cheese), which I figured was enough to keep him occupied until I had bid my farewells.

The Maharishi received me on the small porch attached to his bedroom, and under the supervision of Walter Koch we talked about the prospects for his Spiritual Regeneration Movement and about his hopes for a revival of religious feeling in the West; also about the Vietnam War, which he described as "a nuisance," and about the energy of the American mind, which he thought "so very precious to the world"—the fruit of the tree as opposed to the bark and the branches made manifest among the lesser nations of the earth. More as a formality than in expectation of a straight answer, I asked him a number of questions about the money invested in his organization. He countered each of them with his customary peal of blithe and high-pitched laughter. "Somebody must know about the budgets," he said, "but they're unknown to me." He went on to explain that money is nothing bad and that I should remember that a man wearing a red coat doesn't always know that he's wearing a red coat. Walter Koch could see that I didn't fully grasp the meaning of the observation, and so he filled it out with a number of ideas for the further promotion of the Maharishi's movement, ideas that he thought I might want to mention in the *Saturday Evening Post*—films, posters, Hindu gods and goddesses sold as dolls, two board games (*God-Consciousness* and *Supreme Knowledge*) similar to *Monopoly*, but the second one to be played only by people who had won the first. When a porter appeared to say that the time had come to leave, the Maharishi presented me with a rose. "Mention my love for my master," he said, "I consider myself only the loudspeaker."

On the path leading down to Swaragashram and the river, I met Anneliese and Geoffrey, who gave me a wreath of marigolds and a coin for the ferryman. The color of the sky reminded Geoffrey of El Greco; rain was in the offing, and he wondered if I'd noticed the bruised light like a fresh wound or an open sore at the edge of the western horizon. Knowing that I intended to write about what I'd learned on the ashram, he thought that I'd find it difficult to explain the bright cloud of unknowing to the readers of the *Saturday Evening Post*.

"They won't believe you," he said. "Surely you must understand that?"

I said I did, and Anneliese smiled and pressed my hands, as if I'd said something wonderfully wise. On the way to the ferry I stopped into the Laksmi Café with the thought of saying a last word to O'Shea; neither he nor any of his associates were anywhere to be seen, their absence attributed by Paul Saltzman to some sort of trouble with the police. "A high-ranking federal official from Haridwar," Saltzman said, "who wasn't hip to the ceremonial blowing of the conch."

Where the ferries docked on the Rishikesh side of the river, I found Raghvendra looking out of place and nervous, a gray blanket draped over the white robe that identified him as a monk sworn to the sublime innocence of a child who knows nothing of the world's treachery or commerce. Having been instructed by the Maharishi to make the travel arrangements, he'd thought it prudent to disguise his fear of money. Six people were returning to the world in time—Ringo and Maureen, Marisa Berenson and the Baron de Rosnay, Gypsy Dave, and myself. In New Delhi Raghvendra was obligated to find hotel rooms, book flights to London, Paris, and New York. His hand trembled when he pointed at the two taxi drivers (gold teeth, accommodating smiles, eager to handle the luggage), whom he'd engaged at four times the standard rate.

On the road south the two taxis traveled in close convoy, one never more than a few hundred yards behind the other, and at the frequent stops (for tea and oranges, because the Baron wished to photograph a water buffalo or a leper), we sometimes changed places—Gypsy Dave getting into the car with Ringo, Maureen electing to ride with

Marisa. Raghvendra never moved from the back seat of the lead taxi, not even when it was parked next to a café or a market stall that sold postcards and scraps of gold jewelry. During the whole of the eight hour drive to Delhi he sat with his blanket over his head, humming toneless chants in praise of the Guru Dev.

From time to time I had the chance to talk to Ringo—enroute to Haridwar, at an outdoor table somewhere near Meerut—but I didn't press him for the kind of information that could be changed into news, and I didn't take notes. I remember that he wore bell-bottomed trousers gaudily flecked with black and red stripes, also that I was impressed by his straightforwardness, by his concern for his children, most of all by what I took to be his uncontrived compassion—the feeling unbidden and generous, taking him by surprise—for the people whom he saw on the road bearing their daily burdens of poverty and disease.

He worried about snakes; on the drive north he'd seen one "so big you could see it rising out of its basket in a bazaar," and it reminded him of the photographers lurking around the edges of the ashram, "forever popping out of trees."

His two weeks on the ashram he likened to a stay at a summer holiday camp, along the lines of any number of places in Scotland or the Caribbean except that instead of sailing boats or walking the moors, the campers sat around studying their navels. Which was fine for a few days, but not for much longer, especially when the food wasn't any good and you had to check out the drain for scorpions before getting into a bathtub. George was into Indian ragas, and he probably would stick around longer than John or Paul. John had written a song for Prudence Farrow, hoping to charm her out of her depression, but he was beginning to get irritated by the Maharishi's claims to superior wisdom, by his constant wheedling for money, and by the rumors of his fooling around with the California birds. Nothing to it, of course, anybody who'd seen the Maharishi wouldn't be giving him any points as a film star, but John didn't look kindly upon people who failed to make good on their publicity.

The two taxis reached New Delhi in the late afternoon, and with the well-rewarded assistance of the concierge at the Oberoi Hotel, Raghvendra booked Ringo and Maureen on a plane departing that same night for London. The *Saturday Evening Post* bought dinner for Marisa and the Baron, most of it consisting of strongly curried chicken and well fortified French wine, all of it welcomed by the Baron as proofs of the existence of a world from which he'd been too long absent.

The next day I left for New York, and as the plane lifted over the Punjab in its ascent toward the Khyber pass, the massive bulk of the Himalayan escarpment appeared in the distance to the east, and in my mind's eye I saw Geoffrey and Anneliese waving to me from across the Ganges when I'd come safely to the ferry landing at Rishikesh. On the near shore of the river it had begun to rain, but as Geoffrey had said, the weather that morning was as strange as the light in an El Greco painting, and on the farther shore, clearly visible in the forest of teak and seshum trees, the two figures were standing in bright sunlight, holding flowers in their hands, listening to the voice of the cosmos.

III.

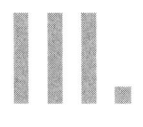

Nearly 40 years later I still can bring the scene vividly to mind, as if it were the long and final camera shot in a fairy tale movie about fantastic elves and minstrels sailing up to the sun until they find the sea of green, and there, at least for a while, live beneath the waves in their yellow submarine. The scene retains its force because I now know that it occurs at almost the precise moment, late February 1968, at which the flood tide of generous thought and optimistic feeling that formed the promise of the 1960's turns on the ebb—toward the assassination of Martin Luther King in April, followed by the assassination of Bobby Kennedy in June, in July by the riots engulfing the Democratic National Convention in Chicago. Another twenty months and the Beatles were no longer together as a band, President Richard M. Nixon was in the White House with his "madman theory" of geopolitics, and cocaine was outselling marijuana on the markets in transcendence. Travel arrangements for magical mystery tours were being handled by the U.S. Army, which over the next six years sent another 35,000 young men to die in Vietnam. By 1972 most of the flowers had wilted, and the psychedelic colors were fading silently to black. But the Beatles had come down from the mountain with the thirty songs recorded on the White Album, among them "Dear Prudence," "Back in the U.S.S.R," and "Revolution No. 9," and in some of the chord changes I can hear the echoes of the Maharishi's laughter and Papageno's flute suspended at a stop in time. More than once I mentioned the effect to Otto Friedrich before he died in 1995. "Bliss consciousness," he said. "The view through the window of eternity."

CREDITS

PHOTOGRAPHS ON PAGES 2-3 AND 16-17 ARE
©NANCY COOKE DE HERRERA/CORBIS
AND ARE REPRINTED BY KIND PERMISSION.

PHOTOGRAPHS ON PAGES 5, 6-7, 18, 22-30, AND
THE BACK COVER ARE BY LARRY KURLAND
AND ARE REPRINTED FROM *THE SATURDAY EVENING POST*.
©1968 SATURDAY EVENING POST SOCIETY/BFLMS.

THE PHOTOGRAPH ON PAGES 8-9 IS REPRINTED
BY PERMISSION OF THE REDFERNS MUSIC PICTURE LIBRARY.

THE PHOTOGRAPH OF MIA FARROW ON PAGE 19
IS ©BETTMANN/CORBIS.

ALL OTHER PHOTOGRAPHS, THOSE ON PAGES 10, 11,
12-13, 14, 15, 20-21, 24, AND THE FRONT COVER ARE
©PAUL SALTZMAN/ WWW.THEBEATLESININDIA.COM
(CONTACT PRESS IMAGES) AND ARE REPRINTED BY
KIND PERMISSION OF THE PHOTOGRAPHER.

THE CAPTIONS USED FOR THE PHOTOGRAPHS ON PAGES
5, 6-7, 18, AND 22-23 ARE REPRINTED FROM *THE SATURDAY
EVENING POST*.

THE CAPTION FOR THE PHOTOGRAPH ON PAGE 19 IS ALSO
ORIGINAL; IT IS REPRINTED FROM THE BETTMANN ARCHIVE.